KT-553-662

Foreword

As Britain's leading short breaks specialist, we clearly recognise the need for detailed information and guidance for you, the would-be traveller. Yet a Citybreak is about more than museum opening times and table d'hôte tariffs, it's a quite sudden and easy submersion in the continental lifestyle – albeit for only a few days.

We were therefore particularly delighted to be able to work with Reg Butler and Settle Press on the City Breaks series. Reg Butler has provided for us a very readable book packed not only with important practical information but with colourful observations in a personal style that captures the very essence of your City Break city.

As well as City Breaks in Paris, you will find on the bookshelves City Breaks in Amsterdam, Rome, Florence and Venice, Moscow and Leningrad, and of course Thomson operate to 18 cities in Europe and the Americas from departure points across the UK.

We're sure you'll find this book invaluable in planning your short break in Paris.

THOMSON CITYBREAKS

Contents

Chapter One

Paris is Always in Season

Paris is always in season, whatever the time of year. Starting from October, one of Europe's biggest Exhibitions, the Paris Motor Show attracts many extra visitors. Then around Christmas and New Year, there are regular visitors from all neighbouring countries, snatching a few days' break to bring the champagne sparkle into winter or to visit the 'Sales'.

Then it's springtime – and *everyone's* heard about the magic of Paris in the Spring. Easter – Whitsun – and it's summer traffic again . . .

Curiously, Paris is 'empty' in August, when the local citizens take off for a month's holiday, surrendering the capital to visitors from abroad. August city traffic is relatively light and jam-free. A car-driver can even find parking space. Many non-tourist shops close for the month.

Whatever the season, all the delights of Paris are awaiting: the pleasures of sightseeing, sitting at boulevard cafés or sampling the great museums; of dining out in colourful restaurants, and revelling in the night-life.

To keep food-and-drink expenses under control, pack a knife and a corkscrew. Central Paris is full of delightful picnic spots alongside the Seine or in the parks. There's no hardship in lunching off a bottle of wine, French loaf, cheese, ham and salad. On a warm day, that kind of lunch can be sheer delight – much more the flavour of Paris than hunting around for a fast-food hamburger franchise. There are hundreds of restaurants that offer a good fixed-price menu, with all details posted outside the doorway. Watch for establishments that are crowded with Parisians shortly after noontime. The locals know best!

To get your bearings, take a city-sightseeing tour by coach. Some tours cover most of the sights in half a day. You can then work out which areas you want to re-visit in more detail; or which museums and galleries you'd like to tackle.

A chapter of this guidebook is headed 'Star highlights – not to be missed'. But don't get yourself fully programmed, morning till night. If you're ticking off a long list of things you want to see, just accept that you probably won't manage to work through them all. Leave some for next time!

It's counter-productive to turn Paris into an assault course. You're in the French capital to enjoy yourself, to get its flavour and enjoy the unexpected. Many pleasures come to the visitor without advance planning. Make time to saunter around, letting each sight capture your attention until another distraction catches your eye.

Refreshment at a pavement café is much more than just a way of quenching thirst or giving your ankles a rest. It's an essential part of the Parisian life-style, enjoying a ringside seat to all the street happenings.

Excursions? For an hour or so, take a Bateaux Mouches boat trip along the Seine; or, one evening, spoil yourself with a luxury-grade dinner cruise to the sound of soft music. For a half-day excursion, Versailles Palace is first choice. If the weather is good, travel out to Fontainebleau, set amid the most beautiful woodlands of France.

It's a popular idea that Paris means Romance. Champagne and flowers can easily be organised to await your arrival at the chosen hotel. Romance isn't just for newly-weds, or couples who are thinking about it. A similar deal can help set the mood for anyone celebrating a silver, gold, ruby or diamond anniversary – much better than spending the money on something sensible like a new tumble dryer.

In fact, to start the trip in truly memorable style, why not go by Orient Express from Victoria, wallowing in 19th-century nostalgia? Here's how the Victorians and Edwardians departed on their Parisian idylls that gave France its champagne-and-oysters reputation.

Mention of Paris normally sparkles the imagination of potential visitors, both male and female. Men may be thinking of nightlife, while the girls probably have shopping in mind.

Both these pursuits can be costly, depending more precisely on what you have in mind.

Night-life is the most dazzling in Europe, from big-time spectacular theatre shows like the Lido, down to off-beat cabaret in dubious clip-joints. If you sample a different cabaret show every night, the supply will hold out for a year.

For a seat close to the stage in top-flight shows like the Lido or the Paradis Latin – where the girls are dressed in ostrich plumes and French perfume – you must book the all-inclusive deluxe dinner arrangement.

There are endless variations on Paris by Night packages. The big advantage is knowing precisely what the evening will cost. Go-it-alone you can have fun, but then be shattered when the final bill is presented.

So much to see – so much to do – the likelihood is that Paris will draw you back. City breaks in Paris never seem to last long enough.

ORIENTATION MAP OF PARIS

Showing *arrondissement* boundaries (indicated by Roman numerals), and the related page numbers of detailed street plans.

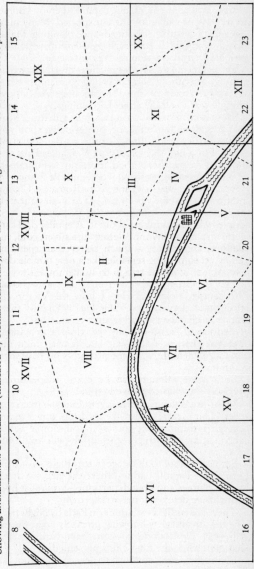

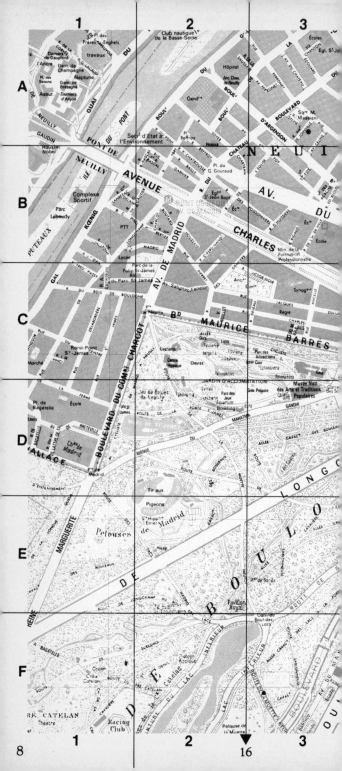

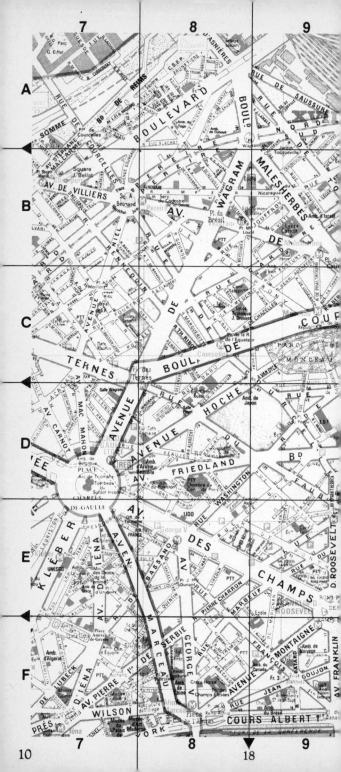

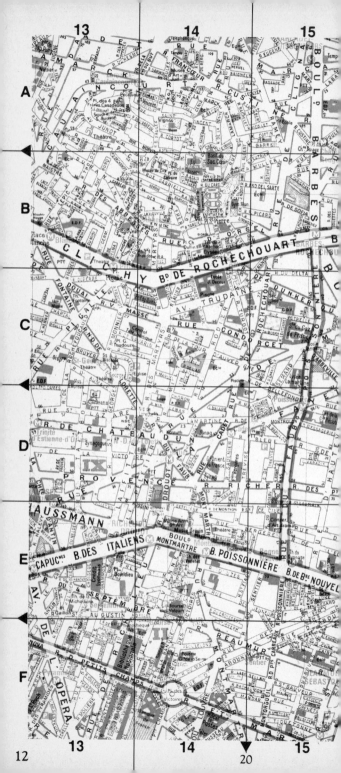

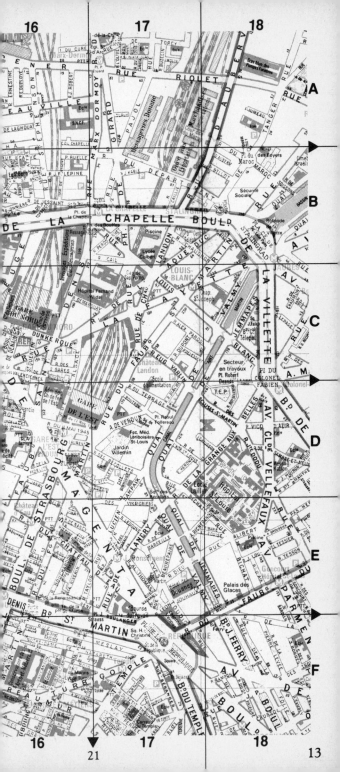

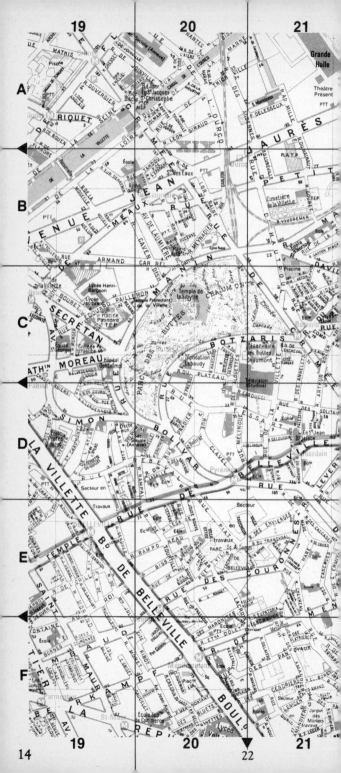

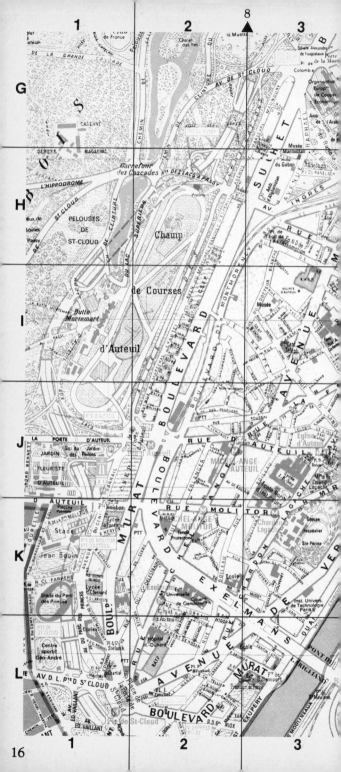

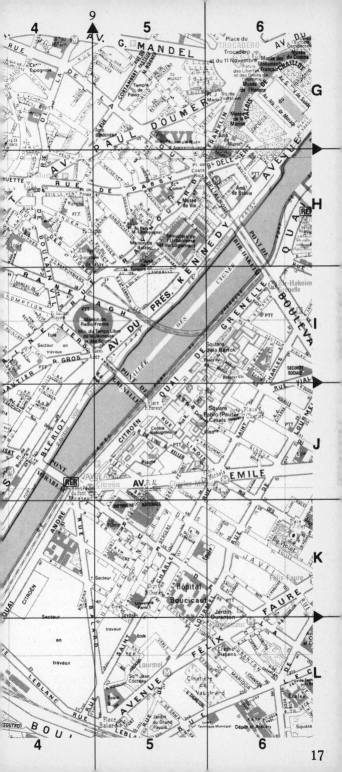

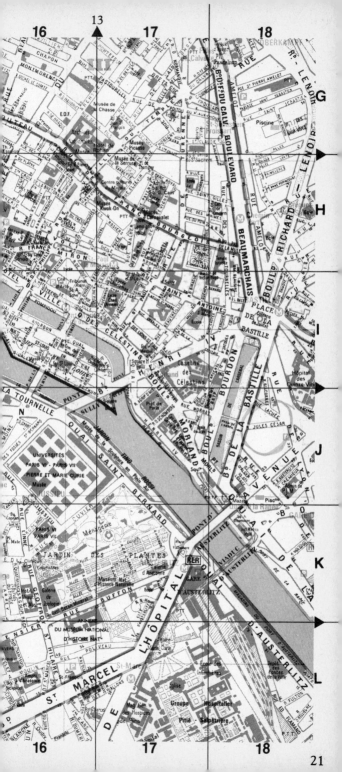

Chapter Two

Your City Break Hotel

Baths and Showers

Many rooms in one star hotels have no bath or shower. If you wish to have a bath ask the reception desk. The bathroom will be prepared for you and towels provided. The charge will usually be about 10 or 12F. (*Bain* is bath, and *salle de bain* is bathroom.)

Breakfast

You will be charged extra at most hotels if you require more than the basic Continental breakfast. You may find it preferable to go to a nearby café if breakfast matters much to you.

Drinks and Minibars

Minibars are becoming more common in higher graded hotels, but check prices as the drinks may be expensive.

Hotels without bars often have a drinks machine, or may sell soft drinks from reception.

Getting in Late

If you arrive back late at night, or in the early hours, and find the hotel door shut, just ring the bell (*sonnerie*) for the night porter (*veilleur de nuit*). Remember that other hotel guests may be asleep when you return.

Lights

Hotel corridors sometimes have a time switch for the lights to allow you enough time to unlock your door. Look for a small orange light and press the button.

In hotel wc's – and also in restaurants, etc. – you will not always find a light switch, as it may operate only when you lock the door.

Safety Deposit Boxes

These are available at most hotels.

Electric voltage

Voltage is 220V (suitable for UK 240V appliances). Plugs

are the standard European two-pin round. Adaptors are easily bought; or fit European plugs to appliances.

Tipping

Service is added to the bill (shown by the letters 's.t.c.' – service and taxes included). There is therefore no need to leave a gratuity.

Nevertheless it is customary to leave a small tip for the chambermaid – say 15 or 20F for a three or four day stay, more if you stay a week (say 25–30F). If the concierge or any other staff have been specially helpful (getting taxis, making telephone enquiries, etc.), they should be given something.

In general, tip for a special service (see chapter twelve on tipping).

Use your discretion: basically, you tip if you want to express your special appreciation at the service.

Day of Departure

You must vacate your room by midday on the day of your departure. The Paris hotel day begins and ends strictly at midday.

The hotel will usually look after your luggage until the time you need to collect it, but if space is difficult don't make unreasonable demands.

Chapter Three

Getting Around Paris

The City Layout

Paris is an easy city to find your way around. The second time you visit it, it will all be in place.

The river Seine flows east to west. North of the river is the Right Bank (*Rive Droite*). South of the river is the Left Bank (*Rive Gauche*).

There are also certain landmarks you will see repeatedly as you move around Paris. The Eiffel Tower is to the west. Montparnasse Tower is to the south, and central in relation to east and west. Montmartre and the white domes of Sacré-Coeur are to the north, also central. Notre-Dame Cathedral is to the east in the centre of Paris.

The Arrondissement System

The key to knowing the location of any place in Paris is the arrondissement system. Arrondissements are districts and Paris is divided into twenty of them. They are arranged in a spiral of three (or more strictly 2½) circular segments going clockwise from the centre.

The centre segment consists of the arrondissements numbered 1 to 7. This is the centre of the old city of Paris. The clockwise spiral starts with the first arrondissement which is approximately centred on the Louvre. For ease of reference, the Louvre may be regarded as the centre of Paris. The 8th arrondissement features the Champs Elysées.

The numbers of arrondissements are written as follows:
1er. lst arrondissement, number for *Premier*.
2e. 2nd arrondissement, number for *Deuxi*ème, (2nd), troisième (3rd), etc. The numbers of arrondissements are indicated in this way in this guidebook.

Public Transport

Paris has an outstanding public transport system. Its underground train service (Métro) is the best in the world. But don't ignore buses which can often prove a more interesting method of travel. A third element in the system is an urban express railway called RER.

Tickets

The same tickets are valid for the Métro and for buses (and also for RER within the city limits).

You can buy tickets singly, but it is much cheaper to buy them in booklets of 10, called *carnets*. Those can be bought from Métro booking halls and at tobacco counters.

Best value is the *Carte Orange* (or orange pass). The Carte Orange is issued free of charge, and it enables you to buy a weekly season ticket (from Monday to Sunday) called a 'Coupon Jaune', or a monthly season ticket (from first to last day of month) called a 'Coupon Orange'. You need to take a passport-size photograph to any Métro station or railway station to obtain the Carte Orange. You must copy the number of your pass (on the plastic holder) on to the 'Coupon' (the season ticket card).

The Carte Orange gives you unlimited travel within Paris on the Métro, buses, and RER.

Possibly most convenient of all for very short-stay tourists, but comparatively expensive, is the 'Paris-Sesame' or Tourist Pass – the Billet de Tourisme. This can be bought from larger Métro stations and mainline railway stations on production of a passport. It is valid from whichever day you choose for either 2, 4, or 7 days. It gives you unlimited travel within Paris on the Métro and RER and on the buses.

Cost (Métro and Bus tickets):

Single ticket	5F (1st class, 6F80)
Carnet (10 tickets)	30F (1st class, 43F)

Carte Orange	
Coupon Jaune (weekly pass)	50F
Coupon Orange (monthly pass)	170F
Tourist Pass (Paris-Sesame)	2 days 57F; 4 days 85F; 7 days 141F.

Métro – Using the System

A Métro map can be obtained from any Métro station. Trains run from 5.30 hrs to 1.15 hr (don't leave your last connection later than 0.30 hrs); one ticket takes you everywhere on the Métro system.

To find your route, proceed as follows:

1) Locate the name of the Métro station you are at on the Métro map.
   Locate your destination and trace the route between the two stations.

2) The Métro lines do not have names as in London. Instead, you travel in the direction of the name of the station at the very end of the line; e.g. if you want to get from Charles de Gaulle-Etoile to Châtelet you would look for signs saying 'Direction Château de Vincennes'.

3) If you need to change lines you repeat the procedure; e.g. from Tuileries to Opéra you would travel to Palais-Royal following the platform signs 'Château de Vincennes' and then to Opéra following the signs 'La Courneuve'. The French for 'interchange' or 'connection' is *correspondance*.

Buses

One ticket covers most journeys across central Paris. But buses differ from the Métro in that you may have to use two tickets for longer journeys within Paris.

Bus stops have their names displayed above them: this is also the name of the immediate area. A clear plan of the bus route is shown inside buses and at bus stops. This means that travelling by bus you can easily keep track of where you are.

On boarding, if you are using a ticket, push the ticket into the machine for punching. If you have a pass – Coupon Jaune, Coupon Orange, or Billet de Tourisme – show it to the driver. Single tickets can be bought on the bus.

27

RER (Express Métro)

This is a rapid way of crossing Paris. There are three RER lines.

There are interchanges between some RER stations and Métro stations. Normal Métro tickets can be used in the central fare stage. You may need to insert your used ticket into a machine to pass through the barriers to change to the Métro or vice-versa.

Taxis

Taxis are not expensive and you need not hesitate to use them in central Paris.

Only taxis displaying the illuminated sign 'Taxi Parisien' are registered taxis. Any other vehicle is not a taxi and may try to charge you an extortionate rate.

There is a meter on the dashboard showing the fare and the rate in use – A, B, or C. The rate increases for night and for out of Paris areas.

Additional charges are made for baggage and for pick-ups from stations and airports.

Most drivers will not take more than three passengers.

On Foot

If you can spare the time the best way to get around Paris is on foot. Paris is a pleasant and rewarding city in which to walk. When crossing roads, however, even at pedestrian crossings, allow for the erratic behaviour of Paris drivers. They have much less consideration than in Britain or the United States.

River Trips

The glass-roofed sightseeing boats are generically referred to as Bateaux Mouches. A Seine river trip is a classic aspect of Paris sightseeing. Boats leave from the right bank (north side) of the Pont de l'Alma, 8e. Cost: 20F or 25F.

Coach Excursions Outside Paris

There are a number of excursions to a wide variety of places within a day or half-day trip of Paris. These excursions provide a guided tour in English. The places include: Chartres, Giverny (home of Monet), Fontaine-bleau, and the Loire Valley.

Chapter Four

The Great Areas

Ile de la Cité

Shaped like a long canal-barge, the Ile de la Cité is one of the two islands that split the Seine. The original Parisii tribe converted this easy river crossing-point into a stronghold, but they couldn't hold out against Caesar. Their island town was burned by the Romans in 52 BC. When the Romans settled in, they built a Palace at the sharp end, and a temple at the other. Centuries later, the Palace was still good enough to house the early kings of France. The site then became the seat of Parliament in the 14th century. Since the Revolution, the buildings were converted to Law Courts – the present-day Palais de Justice. The Conciergerie – north corner of the Palais de Justice – is the sombre jail where over 2500 condemned prisoners awaited transport to the guillotine during the French Revolution. Among them was Marie-Antoinette.

Facing the Law Courts is the Church: Notre-Dame (see chapter five). Climb the north and south towers, up there among the gargoyles, for that fantastic view made familiar by Victor Hugo's *Hunchback of Notre-Dame*. Look down at the central bridges – Pont Notre-Dame and Pont St Michel – which stand where the Parisii settlers built their original wooden bridges to cross the Seine. Just imagine all the comings and goings, across 2000 years of history!

Walk all round the island embankments, looking every direction for a different view. Cross to the *quais* on the 'mainland', and get more pictures of Notre-Dame with foreground bateaux-mouches. Browse among the book-stalls which also sell prints, postcards and general knick-knacks. The entire area is delightful!

Ile Saint-Louis

This is the second of the two boat-shaped islands, 'towed' by the Ile de la Cité, with a small bridge linking the two islands. The atmosphere is quite different: very peaceful, hard to imagine you're in the heart of a big city. Most of the charming town houses were built in the 17th century. Peep into some of the courtyards. Wall plaques remind you of numerous artists, writers and politicians who made Ile Saint-Louis their home. Let's just name Voltaire, Baudelaire, Cézanne.

Walk right round the *quais*, but also turn into the main street called Rue St-Louis-en-l'Ile, with interesting shops including Berthillon's famous ice-cream parlour at no. 31. (See chapter fifteen).

The Louvre and Rue de Rivoli

Start at Place de la Concorde (see chapter five) and stroll through the Tuileries gardens – formal and elegant, with statues everywhere. It's a good spot for a park-bench picnic, if there's room among the mothers and children.

Straight ahead is the Arc de Triomphe du Carrousel, built to celebrate Napoleon's 1805 crop of victories, a vintage year. Beyond is the Louvre. Look back, and you have a dead-straight line through to the Arc de Triomphe: the historic pomp-and-ceremony route.

One side of the Tuileries is the Seine. On the other side are the urbane shop colonnades of Rue de Rivoli, all designed in early 19th century. Stop for a photograph of Joan of Arc, golden on a horse, in the Place des Pyramides.

Saint-Honoré and the 8th arrondissement

This area stretches from Etoile (the huge traffic circle around the Arc de Triomphe), eastwards to Place de la Madeleine. It's a good address, with President Mitterand living in the Palais de l'Elysée, and the British and American Embassies as very close neighbours.

Along the Rue de Faubourg St-Honoré, which runs parallel to the Champs-Elysées, shops cater for the carriage trade. Here is luxury and opulence. It's an experience just to look at the very up-market window displays.

The Opéra Quarter

The Opera itself is among the world's great theatres. Around it swirls the traffic on one of the busiest inter-sections in Paris. Most famous of the café terraces is the Café de la Paix, where thousands of well-heeled tourists write their postcards. Today it's mostly a business district all around, but with plentiful choice of cafés that serve good snacks. It's worth pausing in this area for a light self-service lunch.

Montmartre

In popular imagination, Montmartre became the spirit of Paris. Here were the brilliant artists, the lively women, the cabaret shows and nightlife, the picturesque streets, the zest and the passions and the laughter played out in a captivating setting.

Montmartre is situated on a hill to the north of the centre of Paris: at 423 feet this is the highest point of Paris. It is known as La Butte de Montmartre – *butte* meaning hillock – and Montmartre is often just called La Butte. Montmartre was not incorporated into the city until 1860 and it has retained much of the look of a little town, and also some of the flavour. There are winding cobbled streets, charming little squares and Paris's only vineyard.

The heyday of Montmartre was around the turn of the century, when the painter Toulouse-Lautrec frequented the Moulin Rouge and names like Zola, Degas, Renoir and Van Gogh lived in the area. Its legendary time is past. But the old village is still beautiful, and the area very much alive.

Montmartre has strikingly different aspects to its character. One is that at the foot of the hill is the red light district, around the Place Pigalle and the Boulevard de Clichy. This is also the centre of cabarets and strip shows where the Moulin Rouge and Folies Bergère are still going strong and lend it some real distinction.

The paramount sight of Montmartre is the church of Sacré-Coeur (see separate entry, chapter five). The heart of the old village for tourist purposes is Place du Tertre – very photogenic, still picturesque and replete with café terraces, artists and easels, and musicians.

Note that you can use a Métro ticket on the funicular railway which takes you most way up the hill. If you walk up the Rue Foyatier, you climb 225 steps.

Most people approach from this direction below Sacré-Coeur (Métro: Anvers). An alternative is to take the Métro either to Lamarck-Coulaincourt or Abbesses stations. From there it is fun to wander through the little streets of the village before coming to Sacré-Coeur itself.

Métro: Anvers/Abbesses/Pigalle/Blanche/Lamarck-Caulaincourt.

Les Halles and the Beaubourg

Here, for 850 years, was 'the belly of Paris' – the food market which was exiled in 1979 to a new location near Orly airport. In its place is the Forum des Halles and the controversial Centre Pompidou, otherwise known as Beaubourg. The area has been re-born: the Forum is mostly an underground shopping complex, while the streets around are lively with bars and fast-food, and funky clothing stores.

The Pompidou Centre rates high among the world's most audacious buildings, arousing extreme outrage or admiration. There's nothing like it, anywhere in Europe. Go see for yourself! It's now the top tourist attraction in Paris, leaving the Eiffel Tower cold. (More details, see chapter five). South towards Place du Châtelet, there are numerous late-night jazz bars.

The Marais. 3e and 4e.

The Marais quarter is the oldest area in Paris and provides an intriguing and dramatic difference from the rest of Paris.

It has survived by luck and good fortune. In the middle of the nineteenth century Paris was replanned and rebuilt under the direction of Baron Haussmann. Haussmann's boulevards surround the Marais district, but the Marais escaped being pulled down.

Its streets and buildings are substantially preserved from the Paris of the early seventeenth century. The heart of the Marais quarter is 300 acres of townscape now protected by law.

The Marais extends approximately from the Bastille in the east to the Rue de Temple and the Church of St-Gervais in the west, and from the quais on the Seine to the Rue Pastourelle to the north.

To appreciate it, just wander around the narrow twisting streets. Survey the architecture. Look at the grand mansions and their courtyards, examine the ancient buildings and the carvings above a window.

In the seventeenth century this area was the height of fashion. Some of the grand mansions from that time are open to the public (the French word *hôtel* in this context means town mansion or large house). You should go to the area on a weekday when you can gain access to them. Located near the centre is the Place des Vosges – see chapter fifteen.

Today, the pleasure of the area is not just as a museum piece of townscape. It has a life and charm of today's Paris, with interesting shops and cafés round many an unexpected corner. It is a delightful and wholly successful blend of past and present.

Métro: Hotel-de-Ville/St-Paul/Chemin-Vert/St-Sébastian Froissart/Filles du Calvaire/Temple /Arts-et-Métiers.

The Latin Quarter

Just south of the river from Palais de Justice and Notre-Dame is the Quartier Latin, with cosmopolitan student life based on the Sorbonne – the world's second oldest university after Bologna. It's called Latin Quarter because – until the French Revolution – all teaching was in Medieval Latin, which served like Esperanto for intercourse between different nationalities.

For eight centuries the intellectual and bohemian life-style has flourished. Main street – the ex-Roman road – is Boulevard St-Michel, lined with bookstores and cafés. If you want to be real French, call it Boul'Mich. Here were the big student riots of May 1968. But the area has long since calmed down, particularly since decentralization of the student campuses.

32

The quarter is still home territory for young people of all nationalities. There are any number of cheap and lively ethnic restaurants and cafés. Vibrant activity continues late into the night, with small cinemas, discos, jazz cellars and clubs.

Saint-Germain-des-Prés, 6e

The Left Bank.

Our choice of 'highlights not-to-be-missed' must include an area of the Left Bank. It has to be limited to one area, and the choice falls between the Latin Quarter (5th arrondissement) in the east, the quarters of St-Germain-des-Prés (6th arrondissement) in the middle part and Faubourg St-Germain (7th arrondissement) further west.

For some people – especially the young – it may be that the Latin Quarter will have the edge: it's a focal point for the young, it has an exhilarating feel of youthfulness and openness, it has a colourful look from some of its winding medieval side streets, and there's a lot of activity at all times of day and night.

But we must give the St-Germain-des-Prés quarter precedence: it has the Left Bank atmosphere, and it has Parisian excellence to a very high degree. If you have time to walk around at leisure, this in the eyes of many people is the most attractive area in Paris.

The area lies roughly between the Luxembourg Gardens and the Seine. The church of St-Germain-des-Prés is at its centre. The most distinguished part of it is bounded approximately by Boulevard St-Germain and the river, and Rue des Saints-Pères to the west and Rue de Seine to the east.

Rue Bonaparte and Rue Jacob in particular are streets worth walking every yard if purely for the distinction of the shops. This area is rich in antique shops and galleries, chic dress shops and rare specialist shops. The houses are 17th and 18th century – look into the courtyards and side streets.

There are also interesting old streets and buildings south of Boulevard St-Germain, and the great church of St-Sulpice.

On Boulevard St-Germain, within yards of each other, are perhaps the three best known cafés in the Western world (Café de Flore, Deux Magots, and Lipp). The area is dotted with excellent cafés and restaurants of less fame and a range of prices.

Métro: St-Germain-des-Prés/Rue du Bac/Mabillon.

Montparnasse

On the Left Bank south of St-Germain, Montparnasse was formerly a brilliant international centre of art and bohemian life. Much of that intellectual sparkle now rests in Montparnasse Cemetery, where pilgrims can find the graves of Maupassant, Saint-Saens, Jean-Paul Sartre, Baudelaire and César Franck. A few cafés still manage to keep something of the old atmosphere, but the writers and the expatriates have found other havens.

Champs-de-Mars and Trocadéro

Start from the Champ de Mars, an 18th-century parade ground, close to the Eiffel Tower. For human interest, weekends and Wednesdays the park features puppet-show performances at 3.15 and 4.15 p.m.

Cross the bridge – Pont d'Iéna – and observe the Eiffel Tower framed by trees along the quayside. Then climb up to the Palais de Chaillot, where tour coaches stop on the Place du Trocadéro to a waiting swarm of North African vendors selling souvenirs. From the terrace piazza you can take Eiffel photographs with foreground statuary.

Chapter Five

Star Highlights: Not to be Missed

If you're setting out to see Paris, here are some top priorities.

Arc de Triomphe, 8e
Place Charles de Gaulle

This famous landmark commemorates Napoleon's victories and has been a symbol of French national glory. The Tomb of the Unknown Soldier lies beneath and commemorates the dead of the two World Wars. There is a small museum inside. You can go up to the roof for a marvellous view of Paris.

Open: 10.00-18.00 hrs daily. Cost: 22F by lift or stairs.

Métro: Etoile.

Champs-Elysées, 8e
Avenue des Champs-Elysées

The Champs-Elysées is the most famed street in Europe, and is still around top of the bill for glitter.

A walk along the Champs-Elysées is a requirement for any visitor. At one end is the Arc de Triomphe and at the other end is the Place de la Concorde. The total length is a mile and a half (two kilometres). There are two distinct parts of this great avenue: the division occurs at the traffic island called Rond Point (by Métro station Franklin D Roosevelt).

On the Place de la Concorde side of the Rond Point the avenue is flanked by gardens. West of the Rond Point the avenue rises gently and magnificently to the Arc de Triomphe and it gleams with fashionable cafés and their overflowing terraces, luxurious shops, and cinemas. The wide pavements lined with horse chestnut trees make it a promenader's privilege.

It has inevitably suffered considerably from commercialisation, but the sheer breadth of the avenue and the animation of the human scene along its pavements and shopping precincts keep it well up there as a 'must' not to be missed. But advice to newcomers might be that it is not a place to tarry: it does not have a fetching appeal, and it is expensive.

The Champs-Elysées provides a resplendent setting for Paris at night. Approached from the higher ground of the Arc de Triomphe end, it opens into a brilliant view of the Paris street lamps shining on the banks of a lighted river of traffic. The other view at night from the Place de la Concorde is also magnetising. It confirms the place of the Champs-Elysées as possibly the greatest avenue in the world.

Métro: Etoile/George V/Franklin-D-Roosevelt/
Champs-Elysées-Clemenceau/Concorde.

Concorde, Place de la, 8e.

This vast square was originally laid out in 1755 around an equestrian statue of Louis XV. The royal statue was pulled down during the French Revolution and replaced by the guillotine, which severed the heads of Louis XVI, Marie Antoinette, Danton, Robespierre and over 1300 others. In 1795 the square was named 'Concorde'. The pink granite obelisk of Luxor is from the temple of Rameses II at Thebes in upper Egypt (date 1300 BC) and was erected in 1836 close to where the guillotine had stood. The fountains were created at the same time. The beautiful marble statues of rearing horses that stand where the Champs-Elysées meets the Place de la Concorde are famous; they came from Louis XIV's palace at Marly.

The square should also be seen at night, when it is illuminated by 600 lamps and spotlights. With the Champs-Elysées stretching beyond, here is Paris to be seen as 'The City of Light'.

To the west of the square, you have a view of the Avenue des Champs-Elysées up to the Arc de Triomphe, and in the opposite direction the view extends to the Louvre.

Métro: Concorde.   See also Chapter 15.

Eiffel Tower, 7e

This world-famous structure was built for the Universal Exhibition of 1889, designed as a symbol of the triumph of industrial civilisation and for decades later the tallest in the world. You can take lifts to each of the three stages and there are cafés on the first two. The temptation to be able to say that one's been up the Eiffel Tower is strong and the view is well worth the effort.

A superior way of being up the Eiffel Tower is to have the memorable set lunch at the restaurant on the second stage (separate lift provided). It costs about £22 (tel. 42.26.65.62).

Open: 10.00-23.00 hrs. Monday to Friday and to 24.00 on Saturdays, Sundays and Bank Holidays.

Cost: 1st Floor 12F; 2nd Floor 28F; 3rd Floor 44F.

Métro: Champ de Mars/Trocadéro/Bir-Hakeim.

Notre-Dame Cathedral, 4e
Ile de la Cité

The cathedral of Paris, and very much the city's church. The greatest building in Paris, Notre-Dame is a masterpiece of Gothic harmony. It was built between the 12th and 14th centuries, though most of the marvellous sculptures on the facade are nineteenth century restorations.

The cathedral is nearly always crowded with visitors, but it is not too difficult to take in the main features of the interior. A good overall view is obtained from beneath the great organ at the west end of the nave. For the exterior, besides the view of the west front across the square, go to the gardens on the east and south side, from where there is a clear view of the flying buttresses, the spire and the apse. Regarding a view from the towers, see Chapter 15.

Open: 8.00-17.00 daily.

Métro: Cité.

Sacré-Coeur (basilica), 18e
Rue du Chevalier-de-la-Barre, Montmartre

This church occupies a dramatic setting on the hill of Montmartre (the *Butte*) and it has a commanding view over Paris. Its gleaming white facade with beehive-like domes above are known from countless travel pictures.

For maximum impact, you should approach it from the long flight of steps to the south. A funicular railway will take you part of the way up the hill.

Sacré-Coeur was built by the Catholic church of Paris as a symbol of penitence for the acts of the Paris Commune in 1871, in the wake of the disastrous Franco-Prussian war.

A favourite view of Paris is from its steps (see Chapter 15). The dome is open daily from 6.00 to 22.45 hrs. A visit to the basilica should be combined with an exploration of Montmartre (see Chapter 4).

Métro: Anvers/Abbesses/Lamarck-Caulaincourt.

La Sainte Chapelle, 1er
Boulevard du Palais, l'Ile de la Cité

This chapel has the most glorious and spellbinding stained-glass windows, and the whole chapel conveys a sense of beauty and lightness and transcendence beyond description. Note that the Sainte Chapelle is in fact two chapels: there is a Lower Chapel from which you reach the Upper Chapel by way of narrow, winding stairs. It is the soaring Upper Chapel that is the incomparable masterpiece.

It was built in the thirteenth century and its glass is the oldest remaining in Paris.

Except for its spire topped with a crown of thorns, the Sainte Chapelle is concealed from the outside world as it is hidden away in the precincts of the Palais de Justice.

Open 9.30-18.30 hrs (daily).

Entrance 22F, Students and Seniors 12F.

Métro: Cité.

Galeries Lafayette Department Store, 9e
Printemps Department Store, 9e
Boulevard Haussmann

No new visitor to Paris should overlook these two great department stores which stand next to each other. Ici Paris! The stores are only yards from the rear of the Opéra. Built early this century, the buildings still astonish by their daring. Their exuberant and elegant design is wholly right for their purpose. At street level, they are alight with brilliant window dressing. The quality of the interior decor and ornament is also outstanding. Of special appeal is the Belle Epoque decor of the Au Printemps tea salon beneath a stained-glass rotunda (sixth floor); and in Galeries Lafayette the superb glass and steel dome.

Many claim that Galeries Lafayette is the best department store in the world. Both it and Printemps are unsurpassed. They are beautiful and they are fun; they have unerring style combined with playfulness. They emanate a very Parisian excitement and élan.

Galeries Lafayette and Printemps offer the quickest way of surveying the newest and brightest in the Paris shopping scene, whether in fashion or furniture or household wares. For more on them, see Chapter 8 on Shopping.

Métro: Chausée d'Antin/Opéra/Havre-Caumartin.

The Invalides, 7e

The Hôtel des Invalides was built by Louis XIV in the 1670's as a home for wounded war veterans. It is the largest and possibly the greatest monumental group of buildings in Paris.

The most inspired element in it is the Church of the Dome. The sublime dome is a Parisian landmark and the building is regarded as one of the best examples of the French classical architecture of that era. It is, however, more visited for its tomb than for its architecture.

The tomb is that of Napoleon Bonaparte, whose body was brought here in 1840 from St Helena and certainly has a grandiose resting place.

Les Invalides now houses three museums. The Army Museum (Musée de l'Armée) is one of the best of its kind in the world, with perhaps the largest collection in the world of arms from the medieval period onwards. (See Museums, Chapter 6.)

The other museums are a museum relating to the two World Wars, and a museum devoted to the French Resistance during World War II.

Les Invalides is classical Paris in its full glory. The long facade (645 feet) is perhaps the finest in Paris and looks onto a majestic esplanade stretching down to the Seine.

For the fullest effect and an overall view, you should approach the Invalides from the Alexandre III Bridge. Open: Daily 10.00-17.00 hrs (18.00 hrs in summer). Entrance: 21F.

Métro: Invalides/Latour-Marbourg/Varenne/ Ecole-Militaire.

Museums

On a short stay in Paris it may be impossible to visit each of the major art museums highlighted in this chapter, one can only perhaps pick out those of greatest appeal.

Collections of 'Art', are spread out as follows among the big three national galleries/museums.

The Louvre up to the early 19th century.

The Musée d'Orsay for the nineteenth century and early twentieth century.

The Pompidou Centre's Museum of Modern Art for modern art from early this century until today.

All these museums are described in this chapter together with the Museum of Science, Technology and Industry at the Villette Park on the outskirts of the city.

While you should try to see at least one of these major museums during your stay, you should also remember that Paris has a wealth of other smaller museums which can be enjoyed. For instance, if you haven't been to see the Impressionists at the Musée d'Orsay, you can see some incomparable Monets, together with other Impressionists, in the Musée Marmottan in a delightful house in the quiet of the 16th arrondissement. Or you can see the collection of great Impressionist paintings at the Orangerie, two minutes from the Louvre, where the pictures are more easily absorbed than in a larger museum, and in more pleasurable conditions.

Or if you can't go with your children to the Science City at La Villette, they can see the live scientific demonstrations at the Musée-Palais de la Découverte (Palace of Discovery) in Avenue Franklin-Roosevelt (8e).

The smaller Paris museums certainly cover an extensive and unusual range of interests, including such gems as the Cluny museum, Hôtel Biron (Rodin Museum), Guimet Museum, Picasso Museum, Victor Hugo House, and Hôtel Carnavalet.

The Louvre, 1er

The Louvre has the greatest collection of fine art of any museum in the world. In particular, it is supreme in its collection of paintings. Its size is overwhelming. There are over 200 different galleries, the largest one much longer than a football pitch. What do you do about seeing it?

Here are some suggestions for newcomers.

First, you can look at it from the outside, for it is a former royal palace and is in a magnificent setting. The present vast building has grown in its different parts over the centuries from the Renaissance onwards, and would be worth a good view even if it were empty inside.

Realise that the most you can do at first is to take in a very small sample of the museum. Restrict your ambitions. If there is a part of the collections which particularly interests you, study a plan of the museum and select and see a manageable number of galleries. A good choice of catalogues and maps is available at the entrance and at the bookshop.

If you want to get as good an idea of the Louvre collections as you can on a first visit, the best way is to take a guided tour. Guided tours in English covering the highlights – in fact only some of the highlights – leave frequently (every 20 minutes at peak times) from the ground floor information stand. (A 75-minute tour costs about 22F.)

You will find that the museum is divided into the following main departments: Greek and Roman Antiquities; Oriental Antiquities; Egyptian Antiquities; Sculpture; Objets d'Art and Furniture; Painting; Drawing. It is also in the process of a radical reorganisation of its space, including the building of a vast new underground reception area and service area which will be covered by a striking and controversial pyramid in the Napoleon courtyard. When the redevelopment programme is complete, the visitor's lot will be transformed as well. Meanwhile, it is in a state of transition.

There is a good museum shop which sells reproductions, etc.

Open: Main collection: 9.45-18.30 hrs (other rooms close 17.00 hrs). Closed Tuesdays. Cost: 20F. (Free on Sundays.) Reduced prices for children etc.

Métro: Palais-Royal/Louvre.

Musée d'Orsay, 7e
Quay Anatole France

The new Musée d'Orsay must be securely on the not-to-be-missed list for someone visiting Paris for the first (or umpteenth) time, and as such it is often busy. In terms of both its art collection and its popularity it ranks next to the Louvre among the wealth of Paris museums. Its greatest prize is the world's best collection of Impressionist and Post-Impressionist paintings.

The museum has been a tremendous success since it opened in December 1986. It occupies a converted railway station and station hotel – the station being a marvellous building stunningly restored. It provides a vast area of exhibition space on three floors of galleries and halls.

The museum is devoted to art of the period 1848 to 1914. Most of the best of 19th and early 20th century art from other Paris museums (including the Louvre) has been moved to the Musée d'Orsay. As well as painting and sculpture, it covers the range of 19th century art and design – including photography, architecture, and graphic design.

If you leave the Louvre you need to buy another ticket to get in again on the same day. Here at the Musée d'Orsay you can go in and out during the day on the same ticket.

Open: Tuesday to Saturday: 9.00-17.30 hrs. (Thursday open to 21.15). Sunday: 9.00-18.00; closed Mondays. (June 15 to Sept 15: open 9.00 hrs).
Cost: 23F (12F Sundays). Students and seniors, 12F.

Pompidou Centre – The Beaubourg, 4e

The Beaubourg Centre (as the Pompidou Centre is popularly known) was built as a national centre for modern art and culture in every field. It took off the moment it was opened in 1977, outdoing the Louvre and the Eiffel Tower in the number of visitors it attracted (about 8 million people enter it in a year).

The novel and audacious high-tech appearance of the building is famous. The large Piazza in front of the Centre is the scene of continual acts and 'happenings' by street entertainers and artists. The whole area around buzzes with life.

The Beaubourg building houses the most important collection of modern art in Paris, and in fact the largest collection in the world: the *Musée Nationale d'Art Moderne*. Every important modern painter of the twentieth century is here. The Centre also has special exhibitions of contemporary art.

Entry to the Beaubourg building is free but the museum and major exhibitions have admission charges.

The building has many other multi-media facilities. There is a bookshop with a very extensive selection of postcards and posters on the ground floor. On the top floor is a self-service restaurant with a five-star view – see Chapter 15.

Open: Weekdays (except Tuesday): 12.00-22.00 hrs. Saturday and Sunday: 10.00-22.00 hrs. Closed Tuesday. Cost for Museum of Modern Art: 20F. (18-25 yrs and over-65: 10F.) Sundays free. Day passes available. Entry to building is free.

Métro: Hôtel de Ville/Rambuteau/Châtelet.

La Villette, 18e
Centre for Science and Industry (La Cité des Sciences et de l'Industrie).
Parc de la Villette (at Porte de la Villette).

You may think that there is nothing uniquely Parisian about a science museum – which basically this is.

This may be true – except that there is something particularly French about the imagination and assurance with which this science centre is planned. It qualifies for inclusion here because it is the best museum of its kind.

It opened in 1986. The building is an exciting piece of futuristic architecture. The sheer scale is awesome. It is set in a 74-acre park which is being ambitiously landscaped, with facilities for children, and so on. The displays are designed for active exploration and participation by the visitor. The museum abounds with innovative ideas in presentation.

The permanent exhibition named Explora, for which audio guides in English are available, has four themes: earth and the universe, life and the environment, matter and the work of man, and language and communication. There is an exhibition about the frontiers of French technology, and other attractions and facilities.

There is also the Géode, an enormous 112 foot diameter polished steel sphere which reflects the park in its mirrored walls. It houses a unique cinema with a semi-circular screen covering 10,562 square feet (1000 sq metres).

The exhibitions are in process of being developed further, and so is a whole vast project planned for the Parc de la Villette. It is one of the great enterprises in urban planning in our time.

La Villette is situated on the outskirts of Paris, but there are hours of interest here for anyone with the spark of interest in science and technology and for children for whom there is a discovery and activity centre.

Open: Tuesday, Thursday and Friday: 10.00-18.00 hrs; Wednesday 12.00-21.00 hrs, Saturdays, Sundays and holidays: 12.00-20.00 hrs. Closed Mondays. Cost: 30F; 23F children.

Métro: Porte de la Villette/Porte de Pantin.

Chapter Six

Other Places to See

For convenience, the main buildings/monuments, museums and parks and gardens are listed below by category in alphabetical order.

Buildings and Monuments

Alexandre III Bridge

Built for the 1900 World Exhibition this superb bridge, in the style of the Belle Epoque, was inaugurated by Tsar Alexandre III.

Métro: Invalides.

Arc de Triomphe

See Chapter 5.

Conciergerie, 4e
Quai de L'Horloge

An imposing 14th century Gothic building where you can see the prison cells of Robespierre and Danton and other reminders of the French Revolution.
Open: 9.30-17.30 hrs. Entrance: 22F.

Métro: Cité.

Ecole Militaire, 7e

Regarded by many as one of the finest pieces of 18th Century architecture, this forms the southern boundary of the Champs de Mars. Napoleon received part of his military training here and it is still used by the Army as an officers' training college. It is closed to the public.

Métro: Ecole Militaire.

Eiffel Tower

See Chapter 5.

Fountain of the Innocents, 1er
On the south-east part of the Forum des Halles. Sculpted by Jean Goujon in 1550.

Métro: Les Halles.

The Madeleine, 8e
Place de la Madeleine
Named after St Mary Magdalen and built in the style of a Graeco-Roman temple, this church is particularly lovely at night.

Métro: Madeleine.

Montparnasse Tower
See Chapter 15.

Notre-Dame Cathedral
See Chapter 5.

Opera House, 9e
Designed by Garnier and built in 1875, the Second Empire facade is one of the most famous sights of Paris. The entrance hall and reception rooms can be visited daily. Open: 11.00-16.30 hrs. Entrance: 17F.

Métro: Opéra.

Palais de Chaillot, 16e
Place du Trocadéro
This palace was built in 1937 to house museums and the National Theatre, rather than a monarch. The terrace affords the best view of gardens and fountains of the Trocadéro, the Seine, the Eiffel Tower, the Champs de Mars and the Ecole Militaire beyond.

Métro: Trocadéro.

Palais de Justice, 1er
On the Ile de la Cité opening off the Boulevard du Palais. In the 13th century this was a royal palace but became a court and was renamed during the Revolution. Prisoners from the Conciergerie were brought here for trial. The public are admitted to hearings of civil cases and trials for minor offences. Open: 09.00-18.00 hrs.

Métro: Cité.

The Palais Royal, 1er
Designed in 1639 for Richelieu, it was bequeathed by him to Louis XIII and inhabited by lesser members of the Royal Family. During the Revolution the grounds became the haunt of prostitutes and gamblers. Now it is an area of book and antique shops.

Métro: Palais Royal.

The Panthéon, 5e

Formerly a church, this building became in 1791 a resting place for the 'great men of the days of French freedom'. Among those whose remains are to be found here are Mirabeau, Voltaire, Rousseau, Victor Hugo and Zola.
Open: 14.00-17.30 hrs daily.
Entrance: 22F; students and children 12F.

Métro: Luxembourg.

The Pont Neuf, 1er

The oldest bridge in Paris. Started in 1578 and completed in 1604.

Métro: Pont Neuf.

Sacré Coeur   See Chapter 5.

Church of St Louis des Invalides, 7e

Since 1800, the resting place for famous soldiers. The red sarcophagus of Napoleon is there.
Entrance: 13F.

Métro: Invalides.

Sainte Chapelle   See Chapter 5.

Sewers (Les Egouts de Paris), 7e

Although not strictly a building or a monument, we felt that we could not omit this excursion which departs from Place de la Résistance (7e) at the corner of Quai d'Orsay on Mondays and Wednesdays 14.00-17.00 (and last Saturday of every month), taking you on a guided 'cruise' below the Paris streets.
Entrance: 8F, students and children 4F.

Métro: Alma Marceau.

Museums and Galleries

There are several hundred museums and galleries in Paris and those listed below are merely a selection of some of the most popular and famous.

Most of the museums in Paris offer reduced prices for children, students, under 24's and over 60's. You will need your passport or other identification.

Army Museum, 7e
Hôtel des Invalides

One of the world's richest army museums including many Napoleonic mementoes.
Open: 10.00-18.00 hrs. (Oct.-end March 10.00-17.00 hrs).

Entrance: 21F (reduced price 10.50F every day).

Métro: Varenne.

Cluny Museum, 5e
6 Place Paul-Painlevé
Mediaeval Art – including the beautiful tapestry 'The Lady and the Unicorn'.
Open: 09.45-12.30/14.00-17.15 hrs.
Closed: Tuesdays and Public Holidays.
Entrance: 15F; Sundays 8F.

Métro: St-Michel.

Conservatoire Nationale de Musique, 8e
14 Rue de Madrid
Hundreds of musical instruments including Marie-Antoinette's harp.
Open: Wed-Sat 14.00-18.00 hrs.
Entrance: 7F (Reduced 5F).

Métro: Europe.

Costume Museum (Musée de la Mode et du Costume), 16e
10 Avenue Pierre-1e-de-Serbie
A vast collection of fashion through the ages from 1735 to present.
Open: 10.00-17.40 hrs.
Closed: Mondays and Public Holidays.
Entrance: 20F.

Métro: Iéna.

Decorative Arts Museum (Musée des Arts Decoratifs), 1er
Marsan Pavilion, 107 Rue de Rivoli
Represents all forms of decorative art from the Middle Ages to today, showing the changes in style and taste. Includes design, furniture, tapestries, and arts and crafts.
Open: Wed-Sat 12.30-18.00 hrs, Sunday 11.00-18.00 hrs.
Closed Monday and Tuesday.
Entrance: 20F (Reduced 14F).

Métro: Palais Royal/Louvre.

Grévin Museum, 9e
10 Boulevard Montmartre
The main Paris waxworks, including many historical scenes.
Open: 10.00-19.00 hrs. Entrance: 33F.

Métro: Rue Montmartre/Richelieu-Drouot.

Grévin Museum, Forum des Halles, 1er

A waxworks display portraying the Paris of the Belle Epoque (1885 to 1900). Delightfully done. (A branch of the Grévin Museum above, this is on Level 1 of the Forum.)
Open: 10.30-19.30 hrs. Sunday 13.00-20.00 hrs.
Entrance: 32F.

Métro: Châtelet Les Halles.

Guimet Museum, 16e
6 Place Iéna

Oriental art collection of surpassing excellence and world importance.
Open: 9.45-17.10 hrs., closed Tuesdays.
Entrance: 15F, Sundays 8F.

Métro: Iéna.

The Louvre   See Chapter 5.

Maritime Museum, 16e
Palais de Chaillot

French sea power and shipping through the ages.
Open: 10.00-18.00 hrs.
Closed: Tuesdays and Public Holidays.
Entrance: 18F (Reduced 8F).

Métro: Trocadéro.

Marmottan Museum, 16e
2 Rue Louis-Boilly.

Collection of works by Monet. Also some Empire Rooms.
Open: 10.00-17.30 hrs. Closed: Mondays.
Entrance: 18F (Reduced 8F).

Métro: La Muette.

Musée Carnavalet, 3e
Hôtel Carnavalet, 23 Rue de Sévigné

This museum illustrates the history of Paris over the 400 years from the Renaissance to the Belle Epoque. It also preserves the apartments of Mme de Sévigné, the famous hostess and wit who lived here from 1677-96 during Louis XIV's time. The building itself, in the Marais, is a beautiful and historic mansion.
Open: 9.15-17.40 hrs. Closed Mondays.
Entrance: 12F. Free Sundays. (Reduced 6F).

Métro: St-Paul.

Museum of Mankind, 16e
Chaillot Palace
Illustrates the ways of life of man from different parts of the world.
Open: 09.45-17.15 hrs. Closed: Tuesdays.
Entrance: 15F. Sundays Free.

Métro: Trocadéro.

Orangerie, 1er.
Tuileries Gardens
Beautifully displayed collection of Impressionist and Post-Impressionist paintings.
Open: 09.45-17.15 hrs. Closed: Tuesdays.
Entrance: 15F. Sundays 8F.

Métro: Concorde.

Musée D'Orsay
See Chapter 5.

Palais de la Découverte, 8e
Grand Palais
Museum of scientific discoveries and a planetarium. Live demonstrations of many aspects of popular science.
Open: 10.00-18.00 hrs. Closed: Mondays.
Entrance: 15F (Planetarium 11F extra).

Métro: Franklin D Roosevelt.

Petit Palais, 8e
Avenue Winston Churchill
Museum of fine arts, renowned for its outstanding contemporary exhibitions.
Open: 10.00-17.40 hrs. Closed: Mondays.
Entrance: 12F.

Métro: Champs Elysées-Clemenceau.

Picasso Museum Hôtel Salé, 3e
5 Rue de Thorigny
Works of Picasso – Picasso's own collection.
Open: 09.15-17.15 hrs, Wednesday till 22.00.
Entrance: 21F.

Métro: St Paul/Chemin Vert.

Pompidou Centre
See 'Highlights', chapter five.

Rodin Museum, Hôtel Biron, 7e
77 Rue de Varenne
Rodin's sculptures in a lovely mansion and garden.

Open: 10.00-17.45 hrs. Closed: Tuesdays.
Entrance: 16F.

Métro: Varenne.

Victor Hugo Museum, 4e
6 Place des Vosges.

Mementoes of the author's life and works including sketches for the 'Notre Dame de Paris' manuscripts.
Open: 10.00-17.40 hrs.
Closed: Mondays and Public Holidays.
Entrance: 9F.

Métro: Bastille.

Parks and Gardens

Bois de Boulogne
Over 2000 acres woods, lawns, boating lakes, amusement parks, zoo, racecourses, restaurants.

Métro: Les Sablons.

Bois de Vincennes
Slightly further out of town but worth a visit if the weather's good: lake, woods, park, zoo, racetrack, Indo–Chinese garden.

Métro: Château de Vincennes.

Botanical Gardens (Jardin des Plantes), 5e
Include a winter garden, an alpine garden, a menagerie of various birds, beasts and reptiles and over 10,000 classified plants. An entrance fee to various sections may be charged. The Natural History Museum is on the same site.

Métro: Gare d'Austerlitz/Jussieu.

Luxembourg Gardens, 6e
The most extensive green open space on the Left Bank.

Métro: Luxembourg.

Palais Royal, 1er
Elegant walled garden.

Métro: Palais Royal.

Parc Monceau, 8e
Landscaped garden with many statues and trees based on an English garden.

Métro: Monceau.

Tuileries Gardens, 1er
Lovely, typically French formal gardens.

Métro: Tuileries.

Cemeteries

Père-Lachaise cemetery, 20e
A huge town cemetery with 19th and 20th century tombs, some old and crumbling, others wildly imaginative. This is the resting place of many famous names: Chopin, Molière, Racine, Oscar Wilde, Proust, to name but a few.

Montmartre cemetery, 18e
Other famous people rest here, including Baudelaire, Stendhal, Berlioz.

Chapter Seven

Out of Paris:
Trips to Surrounding High Spots

Most tour operators offer day excursions to a number of the following high spots. This is an informative and hassle-free way of visiting them.

Versailles
13 miles south-west of Paris
The palace of Versailles and its gardens and park is the world's most sumptuous royal residence. It was built by the Sun King, Louis XIV, between 1661 and 1682.

The sheer scale and grandeur are overwhelming. The roof area of the palace is 27 acres; the gardens are 235 acres, with a park of 14,000 acres beyond.

One could spend a profitable day in the superbly landscaped and ornamented gardens without setting foot in the palace. But at least you must see the State Apartments of the King and Queen, the Hall of Mirrors and some of the private rooms.

There are guided tours in English. Open daily: Palace, 9.45-17.00 hrs, Gardens, dawn to dusk.

Fontainebleau
40 miles south-west of Paris

Fontainebleau is another royal palace, lovelier than
Versailles if less majestic. The core part of the château
complex was built by François I in the 16th century, but
later monarchs in the 17th and 18th centuries added to it.
The result is a rich variety of styles which allows one to see
the evolution of French architectural design and interior
decoration. The François I Gallery was decorated by
leading Italian Renaissance artists and should not be
missed. Also see the boudoir of Marie-Antoinette, which
is a most exquisite room.

Fontainebleau is often much less crowded than Versailles,
and guided tours are available.

Around the palace is the forest of Fontainebleau –
42,000 acres of woodland in a remarkable setting of
dramatic rock formations. The forest in itself merits a full
star rating.

Palace open daily 9.30-12.30, 14.00-17.00 hrs; closed
Tuesdays.

Vaux-le-Vicomte, Château de
31 miles south-east of Paris (near Melun)

One of the great classical châteaux of France, with gardens
of equal quality. Vaux offers the entrancing delight of the
French country house at its best.

Open April to October; 10.00-18.00 hrs; in winter,
weekend afternoons only; closed in January.

Chantilly
26 miles north of Paris

Beautiful château, splendid art collection with great
masterpieces (Musée Condé), and surroundings of a fine
park.

Also the famous racecourse. 3000 thoroughbreds train
here each year. The 18th century stables are now the
Living Museum of the Horse (Musée Vivant du Cheval),
showing different breeds in the flesh and giving equestrian
demonstrations, and also displaying objects related to
horses. A treat for the horse enthusiast.

Park and museums open daily, 10.00-18.00 hrs; closed
Tuesdays.

Giverny
50 miles north-west of Paris

Monet's house, and the garden immortalised in his
paintings.

Open April to end October. Closed Mondays.

Entrance to house 10.00-12.00 hrs, 14.00-18.00 hrs.

Chartres
55 miles south-west of Paris

Well worth the journey, to see one of the greatest cathedrals of the Middle Ages. After your visit, explore the narrow hilly streets, and make time for the stained-glass centre at 5 rue de Cardinal Pie. (Centre International du Vitrail – open 10.00-18.00 hrs, closed Tuesdays.)

Chapter Eight

Shopping

Paris is one of the greatest shopping centres in the world – and it comes top as the most seductive. Here shopkeepers from the most modest to the grandest can create that special allure.

Shopping and window shopping are likely to be one of the high points of any visit to Paris. The Parisian sense of display is a perpetual delight, and some of the window dressing reaches ravishing heights. Glamour is in the air. More earthily, you can enjoy the exuberance and character of the markets.

The most typical and inimitable aspect of Paris shopping is the number of small shops of individuality. There are also grand department stores, but it is the range and character of its boutiques that gives the special style and colour to this great garden of shopping.

Prices

The articles in many Paris shops are frequently more expensive than in Britain or America, but offer good value if you know where to look. Often you'll feel it's worth paying the higher price for quality, fashion or design. Many shops will gift-wrap at no extra charge.

Sizes

For women's dresses and suits, these are sizes for the equivalent French, British and American measurements.

France	36N	38N	40N	42N	44N	46N	48N
Britain	10	12	14	16	18	20	22
USA	8	10	12	14	16	18	20

Fashion and Clothes

For women's fashion, shopping in Paris still ranks first in the world.

Haute Couture

The highest pinnacles of women's fashion are the *grands couturiers*, the great designers and dress makers of *haute couture*. Two streets near the Champs-Elysées house many of the famous names: the Avenue Montaigne (includes Christian Dior, Guy Laroche, Nina Ricci), and the Rue du Faubourg Saint-Honoré. Most of the other supreme names – Balmain, Ted Lapidus, Chanel, etc. – are in streets within ten minutes' walk of these two streets, in particular Rue François 1er, Avenue George V, and some side streets.

These haute couture houses also have boutiques, usually on the same premises, where you can buy handmade ready-to-wear clothes – at phenomenal prices. But walk around, look, and be enthralled.

Avant Garde styles

For avant garde designers, the hottest centre is the Place des Victoires (2e), near Les Halles. There are many exciting boutiques in Les Halles area. Another area which is a bright centre of new design is in Saint-Germain-des-Prés on the Left Bank, especially the boutiques in the area round Rue de Grenelle and Rue du Cherche-Midi (7e. Métro: Sèvres-Babylone, or Rue du Bac or St-Germain-des-Prés).

More fashion shopping

There are original and beguiling boutiques all around Paris.

If you want to look at the new fashions, don't forget the great department stores, Galeries Lafayette and Printemps, described in Chapter 5 and below under 'department stores'.

Bargain and Discount Stores

Paris has more and better shops specialising in discount and secondhand clothing of quality than any other city in Europe. Many of these shops deal in designer clothes at far below their original price.

Last season's stock from fashion houses may sell at half price. If you see the word *dégriffés*, it means 'without label', and they will be designer garments heavily discounted.

Also look for the word *Soldes*: it means bargains or reductions.

There are two streets on the Left Bank which are lined with shops specialising in bargains – *dégriffés* and *soldes*.

Here you may get classy clothes on the cheap. The streets are:

Rue Saint-Placide, 6e. Métro: St-Placide.

Rue Saint-Dominique, 7e. Métro: Latour Maubourg/Invalides.

Paris is also well supplied with upmarket secondhand clothes shops.

For the visitor, the easiest secondhand shop for buying clothes is probably Reciproque, at 95, 101, and 123 Rue de la Pompe, 16e. (Do investigate all three shops if you go.) Métro: Pompe/Victor Hugo.

Another strong tip for the visitor interested in high quality secondhand clothing – for women, children and men – is, Chercheminippes, 109-111 Rue du Cherche-Midi, 6e. Métro: Vaneau.

Some Interesting Shopping Streets and Places

Forum des Halles, 1er.

Métro: Les Halles/Château-Les-Halles.

The Forum is a pedestrian concourse of glass and aluminium which descends to four levels. Because of the design, all levels get natural light. It was opened in 1979 as a shopping and leisure complex. A great variety of shops (over 200), 12 cinemas, many cafés and restaurants, around lively arcades. Very popular, plenty to see, and no need to take account of the weather above. A good place to look for presents. The area around is blooming too.

Rue Bonaparte. Also Rue des Saints Pères, 6e.

(Métro: St-Germain-des-Prés).

An excellent area for exotic antiques. Also high fashion boutiques. Good window shopping.

Rue du Paradis, 16e.

Métro: Châteaud'Eau/Poissonnière

Lined with shops for porcelain, glass and table ware – makes quite an astonishing display. Includes the great Baccarat establishment who have a dazzling collection of glass objects in a museum (Musée du Cristal) at No 30.

Department Stores

The large department stores have information desks where English is understood.

Galeries Lafayette and Printemps.
Boulevard Haussmann, 9e.

Métro: Chausée d'Antin/Havre-Caumartin/Opéra See also Chapter 5.

These stores keep at the leading edge of Paris shopping. Marvellous for fashion (the Galeries devotes two floors to its fashion department, and more than 10,000 customers visit it every day), lingerie, perfume and cosmetics, jewellery, glass and porcelain. Exciting for furniture and design – Printemps ahead in this field. Excellent too for toys (especially Printemps), children's accessories, household items – and presents. The displays are of museum quality.

Although not cheap, prices are not excessive. Try to visit them weekday mornings when they are less crowded. Avoid Saturdays when they are madly swarming with shoppers. Rest your feet with a coffee on the top floor and a fine view of Paris.

English is spoken by the staff in these shops.

Aux Trois Quartiers,
17 Boulevard de la Madeleine, 1er.
Métro: Madeleine.
Attentive service and high quality goods. Has the great advantage of not being crowded. Expensive, but you can shop here in calm and comfort. Staid in manner, conservative in merchandise, very reliable. Relaxing *salon de thé* on 4th floor. (Men's dept. Madelios, next door.)

Au Bon Marché, 38 Rue de Sèvres, 7e
Métro: Sèvres-Babylone
A real department store, the oldest one in Paris, and the only major one on the Left Bank. Has a superlative self-service food hall. Covers most shopping requirements at moderate prices. Also has an antiques department. Not very crowded.

La Samaritaine, 75 Rue de Rivoli, 1er.
Métro: Pont Neuf/Châtelet
An enormous family-type department store in four huge buildings. Highly regarded particularly for practical clothes and working clothes and household items. Realistic or low prices. Open on Wednesdays until 10 p.m.

Supermarkets

Monoprix, Prisunic and Uniprix are chains of supermarkets with several outlets throughout Paris. A good selection of food and wine, clothes, cosmetics, and household items, at reasonable or cheap prices and surprising quality. Larger branches stock many items suitable for presents.

Branches of Nicolas carry a wide variety of wines and spirits.

Markets

Markets abound in Paris and are part of Paris life. There are open air markets selling antiques, or stamps, or flowers, and much else. But above all, there are markets for food.

Street Food Markets

Every visitor to Paris should go to a street food market to get an insight into a fascinating aspect of the Parisian lifestyle.

Early morning is the best time to visit food markets. The sellers have set up their stands by 8 a.m., they stop at 13.00 hrs, and they re-open at around 16.00 hrs until 19.30 hrs. Nearly all markets are closed on Mondays; some are closed on Sundays; other are open Sunday mornings.

Wherever you are staying in Paris, there will be a market in your neighbourhood. It may be as interesting as those which are more famous. Following are some well-known markets.

Rue Cler, 7e
Tuesday to Saturday

Bustling with vitality – a fine example of a Parisian street market, though distinctly classy. Runs from Avenue de la Motte-Picquet to the Rue de Grenelle. Near The Invalides and the Eiffel Tower.

Métro: Ecole Militaire.

Rue de Buci and Rue de Seine, 6e
Tuesday to Sunday

The most photographed street market and the most colourful. Very entertaining.

Métro: St-Germain-des-Prés/Odéon.

Rue Mouffetard, 5e
Tuesday to Sunday

Extends from the Rue de l'Epée de Bois to the Carrefour des Gobelins, near the Latin Quarter. Explore the side streets as well.

Métro: Censier Daubenton/Monge.

Flower Markets

There are three special flower markets and they provide enchantment for the eyes and nose. Locations are:

Place Lépine, Ile de la Cité, 1er

This is the most famous flower market, situated near

Notre Dame on the Ile de la Cité.
Open 8 a.m. to 7 p.m. Monday to Saturday. (On Sundays the Place Lépine becomes a bird and pet market.)

Madeleine Flower Market, 8e
This is held at the back of the Madeleine and is open daily except Mondays.

Place des Ternes, 17e. (Métro: Ternes.)
Also has an excellent food market.
Open Tuesday to Sunday.

Flea Markets

The flea markets (*marchés aux puces*) have been a well known feature of Paris. The days when they offered plenty of bargains are long since gone.
   Three of the most noteworthy ones are:

Marché aux Puces de Saint-Ouen, at Porte de Clignancourt, 18e
Open Saturdays, Sundays, and Mondays, 7 a.m.-7 p.m.
   If you go only for entertainment value, this is as good a choice of flea market as any. It is the largest flea market in Europe extending for 6½ kilometres (4 miles), so you won't see it all in one visit. Lots of junk, lots of antiques, lots of tourists, and lots of atmosphere.

Métro: Porte de Clignancourt.

Porte de Vanves, 14e.
Av Georges Lafenestre and Av Marc Sangnier
Saturdays and Sundays 7 a.m.-1 p.m.; some vendors to 7 p.m.
The Avenue Marc Sangnier has a good and cheap market for bric-à-brac. Round the corner in Avenue Lafenestre is the quality part of the market.

Métro: Porte de Vanves.

Porte de Montreuil
Saturdays and Sundays 7 a.m.-7 p.m.
A pleasant market to wander around. The best flea market for secondhand clothes, including fashionable clothing from long ago.

Métro: Porte de Montreuil.

Chapter Nine

Eating and Drinking

Paris is the gastronomic capital of the world. In no other city can be found such a good choice for eating out with real enjoyment. Moreover you will get better value for money than say in Britain, as standards in modest restaurants are much higher and prices are moderate.

Eating and drinking places in Paris can be classified as follows:

Restaurants: These are for proper meals (that is lunch and dinner). Prices range from very cheap to very, very expensive. (Very small restaurants are also called 'bistros'.)

A *brasserie* is part restaurant, part café – essentially it is a grander café.

Cafés are generally open all day, starting by serving coffee and croissants for breakfast. They will serve a more or less limited range of food (sandwiches, snacks, etc.), and some offer a main meal, usually one *plat du jour*. They serve a wide variety of hot and cold drinks and wines, spirits, and beer. They generally have both a bar counter and tables.

Café-tabacs are a variety of café which also sells tobacco, stamps, postcards, Métro tickets, etc., and are generally cheap. They have a maroon diamond-shaped sign outside.

Fashionable cafés can be very expensive.

Bars: There is no real distinction between most 'bars' and 'cafés' – the names cover the same kinds of places. However, some bars have a distinctly smart, cocktail-style character and may have live music during the evening. These we will call *Smart Bars*, and they will be considered separately in the next chapter on 'Nightlife and Entertainment'. They are sometimes described as 'American bars'.

Wine bars are also quite distinct from other café-bars.

There are a few 'pubs' and beer cellars serving beers on draught.

The small number of *salons de thé* (tea rooms) usually open mid-mornings for cakes and snacks. Most also serve wine. They are rather upmarket and usually quite pricey.

The *Selfs* are self-service restaurants or cafeterias.

For take-away food, use the traditional French outlets.

Traiteur (delicatessen) and *charcutier* (prepared meats) shops will offer a variety of interesting snacks and ready-to-eat dishes (*plats cuisine*). *Boulangeries* and *pâtisseries* (bread and pastry shops) are open until 7 p.m.

Restaurants

Initial Advice

If you don't want a full meal, go to a café (or crêperie, cafeteria, etc.), not to a restaurant.

Prices are always displayed outside every restaurant. The word *menu* in France means a set meal of more than one course with limited or no choice of dishes. A la carte refers to individually priced dishes any of which you may choose. Examine the prices and the choice of *menus* and *à la carte* dishes before you walk in.

It is almost invariably much cheaper and better value to choose the fixed price menu (*menu prix fixe*) than to eat *à la carte*. You may be charged extra if you change an item on this menu, even a vegetable. On the other hand, opting for *à la carte* will offer you much greater choice, but the *plat du jour* is often the best choice in more modest restaurants.

You can always have a jug of drinking water from the tap free in any restaurant or café (ask for *une carafe d'eau*. Sometimes wine or mineral water is included in the *menu prix fixe*. Remember extras can mount up surprisingly.

Respect the waiter, but do not be diffident. Address him or her politely as 'monsieur' or 'mademoiselle', and ask for advice whenever you want it. Service is slower and meals more leisurely in France than is generally the case in Britain and America. You may wait for a dish to be freshly prepared.

A compulsory service charge of 15% is included in the advertised price of all restaurants and cafés in Paris. It is at your discretion whether you wish to leave an extra tip, normally up to 10% is expected.

Many restaurants close on Sundays or Mondays in August. At the better known/expensive establishments, it is advisable to book a table in advance, particularly at weekends.

Selection of Restaurants

You will find restaurants around practically every corner and down most side streets. A good proportion of them are commendable.

Following is a short selection of restaurants from each arrondissement which we can recommend.

Regarding prices: you can spend more or less money in a restaurant according to your choice. Because of this, we have adopted a grading system which allows for a recommended complete meal.

£ = under £10 and frequently a lot less.
££ = £10–£20.
£££ = £20+

A list of restaurants follows:

1e Arrondissemont

Yakitori   34 Place du Marché St Honoré
Tel. 42 61 03 54   Métro: Tuileries
Open until 22.45
Traditional Japanese brochettes.   £

Le Bistro d'Hubert   36 Place du Marché St Honoré
Tel. 42 60 03 00   Métro: Tuileries
Open until 22.00 hrs. Closed Sundays.
Excellent traditional cuisine.   £

Le Petit Goulot   20 Rue du Roule
Tel. 42 36 72 52   Métro: Châtelet/Louvre
Open 12.00-14.30/19.00-22.30 hrs (not Sun & Mon)
Generous helpings, traditional cooking.   £

Les Bouchons   19 Rue des Halles
Tel. 42 33 28 73   Métro: Châtelet
Open 12.00-01.00 hrs
1920s decorphere. Brunch served until 15.00 hrs.   ££

2e Arrondissement

Le Drouot   103 Rue de Richelieu
Tel. 42 96 68 23   Métro: Richelieu-Drouot
Open until 21.30
  Excellent value, very French, very popular.   £

Vichnou   Rue Daunou/Volney
Tel. 42 97 56 54   Métro: Opéra
Open 12.00-14.00 hrs, 19.00-23.00 hrs. Closed Monday
a.m.
  Superb atmosphere and excellently prepared Indian
dishes.   ££

Le Vaudeville   29 Rue Vivienne
Tel. 42 33 39 31   Métro: Bourse
Open 11.00-15.00 hrs, 19.00-02.00 hrs.
  1920s style traditional cuisine, oysters and fresh foie
gras.   £££

4e Arrondissement

Le Canaille   4 Rue Crillon
Tel. 42 78 09 71   Métro: Sully Morland
Open 11.45-14.15 hrs, 19.30-23.00 hrs (Closed Sat/Sun
midday)
  Old Bistro Style, set three course menu, usually
busy.   £

Le Tour Tour   20 Rue Quincampoix
Tel. 48 87 82 48   Métro: Châtelet/Les Halles
Open 12.00-14.30 hrs, 19.00-00.30 hrs.
   Good food, lively background music. Jazz bar and
theatre downstairs.   £

Le Quincambosse   13 Rue Quincampoix
Tel. 42 78 68 48   Métro: Châtelet/Les Halles
Open Daily until 23.00
   Simple cooking, good quiches and salads attractively
presented.   ££

Bofinger   7 Rue de la Bastille
Tel. 42 72 87 82   Métro: Bastille
Open daily until 01.00 hrs
   Authentic art nouveau style brasserie. Traditional
French, seafood and fish.   ££

Taverne du Sergeant Recruteur
41 Rue St Louis en l'Ile
Tel. 43 54 75 42   Métro: St Paul/Pont Marie
Closed Sunday.
   Limitless wine and starters.   ££

Les Caves du Marais St Cathérine   5 Rue Caron
Tel. 42 72 39 94   Métro: St Paul
Closed Mondays and Tuesdays lunchtimes.
Intimate cellar restaurant, candlelight and classical music.
Excellent hors d'oeuvres buffet.   ££

5e Arrondissement

La Ferme St Geneviève
40 Rue de la Montagne St Geneviève
Tel. 43 54 49 85   Métro: Maubert Mutualité
Open daily, closed Monday lunchtime.
Regional specialities, simple cooking.   £

Le Grenier de Notre Dame   18 Rue de la Bûcherie
Tel. 43 29 98 29   Métro: St Michel
Open 12.00-14.30 hrs, 19.00-22.45 hrs, closed Tuesday.
One of the best vegetarian restaurants.   £

Le Caprice de Monge   107 Rue Monge
Tel. 43 36 08 03   Métro: Censier Daubenton
Open Daily 12.00-15.00 hrs, 19.00-
23.00 hrs.   £

Le Blé en Herbe   8 Rue Mouffetard
Tel. 43 25 46 88   Métro: Monge/Cardinal Lemoine
Evenings only. Closed Tuesday.
Traditional French food.   £

L'Atelier Maître Albert   1 Rue Maître Albert
Tel. 46 33 06 44   Métro: Maubert Mutualité
Open until midnight, closed Sunday.
A beautiful fireside setting. Excellent
cooking.   ££

La Cochonaille   21 Rue de la Harpe
Tel. 46 33 96 81   Métro: St Michel
Open daily until 23.30 hrs
Traditional restaurant with a wide choice of
menus.   ££

6e Arrondissement

La Cour St Germain   156 Bd St Germain
Tel. 43 26 85 49   Métro: St Germain des Près
Open daily until 00.30
Interesting starters, mouth-watering desserts and steaks.
Excellent value.   £

Restaurant des Beaux Arts   11 Rue Bonaparte
Tel. 43 26 92 64   Métro: St Germain des Près
Open daily until 23.00 hrs
Excellent value! Haunt of many a student and
artist.   £

L'Assiette au Beurre   11 Rue St Benoît
Tel. 42 60 87 41   Métro: St Germain des Près
Open daily 12.00-15.00, 19.00-23.00
Good value, popular and noisy.   ££

Closerie de Lilas   171 Bd Montparnasse
Tel. 43 26 70 50   Métro: Port Royal
Open daily until 01.00 hrs
Hemingway used to eat here! Renowned for its
seafoods.   ££

Les Jardins St Benoit   20 bis Rue St Benoît
Tel. 42 22 48 10   Métro: St Germain des Près
Open daily until midnight.
Very good food, well presented in a pleasant
setting.   ££

Brasserie Lipp   151 Bd St Germain
Tel. 45 48 53 91   Métro: St Michel
Open 12.00-00.45 hrs, closed Monday and July.
Classical Brasserie. Traditional meeting place of
politicians and academics.   ££

7e Arrondissement

La Petite Chaise   36 Rue de Grenelle
Tel. 42 22 13 35   Métro: Sèvres-Babylone
Open daily. Serves until 22.30.
A fashionable, eighteenth century style
restaurant.   ££

Leo Le Lion   23 Rue Duvivier
Tel. 45 51 41 77   Métro: Ecole Militaire
Open 12.30-14.00 hrs, 19.30-22.30 hrs.
Closed Sat and Sun in November/December
Excellent cooking from the Lyon region of
France.   ££

Le Petit Niçois   10 Rue Amélie
Tel. 45 51 83 65   Métro: La Tour Maubourg
Open until 22.30 hrs.
Closed Sunday and Monday midday.
Friendly atmosphere, good fish.   ££

8e Arrondissement

L'Assiette au Boeuf   123 Av des Champs Elysées
Tel. 47 20 01 13   Métro: Charles de Gaulle-Etoile
Open until 01.00.
Basic menu at reasonable prices.   £

Le Cellar   38 Rue de Ponthieu
Tel. 43 59 25 28   Métro: Franklin D Roosevelt
Open Monday to Saturday until 01.00.
Friendly atmosphere. Good food. Pianist and Singer from
21.00.   £

La Rotonde   12 Place St Augustin
Tel. 45 22 33 05   Métro: St Augustin
Open daily.
Art Deco interior. Meat and seafood
specialities.   ££

Le Salardais   2 Rue de Vienne
Tel. 45 22 23 62   Métro: St Augustin
Closed Sat and Sun Midday.
Traditional French cuisine. Menu includes
wine.   ££

Boeuf sur le Toit   34 Rue du Colisée
Tel. 43 59 83 80   Métro: Franklin D Roosevelt
Open until 02.00 hrs.
Spectacular Art Deco interior. Excellent
seafood.   £££

Café du Roy   Rue Royale
Métro: Concorde/Madeleine
Open daily.
Elegant restaurant with delicious food and
wines.   £££

9e Arrondissement

Chartier   7 Rue du Faubourg-Montmartre
Tel. 47 70 86 29   Métro: Rue Montmartre
Open until 21.30 hrs
A nineteenth century 'bouillon' (popular restaurant)
delightfully preserved. Food is basic and cheap. A lively,
entertaining restaurant.   £

Chez Maurice   44 Rue Notre Dame de Lorette
Tel. 48 74 44 86   Métro: St Georges
Open daily until 23.00 hrs.
Good French cooking.   ££

Charlot   12 Place de Clichy
Tel. 48 74 49 64   Métro: Clichy
Last orders for food 23.30 hrs.
Pricey but one of Paris' best shellfish restaurants. Must
reserve.   £££

10e Arrondissement

La Taverne de la Bière   15 Rue de Dunkerque
Tel. 42 85 12 93   Métro: Gare du Nord
Open until 02.00 hrs, last orders 23.30.
Huge selection of beers. Good sauerkraut and typically
French and Alsatian food.   £

Terminus Nord   23 Rue de Dunkerque
Tel. 42 85 05 15   Métro: Gare du Nord
Open daily until 01.30 hrs.
1925 Brasserie, specializing in oysters, seafood and sauerkraut.   £££

Julien   16 Rue du Faubourg St Denis
Tel. 47 70 12 06   Métro: Strasbourg St Denis
Open 12.00-15.00 hrs, 19.00-01.30 hrs
Brasserie style with Art Nouveau interior. Excellent food,
speciality fish.   £££

Chez Flo   7 Cour des Petites Ecuries
Tel. 47 70 13 59   Métro: Strasbourg St Denis
Open daily until 02.00 hrs.
Famous restaurant. Excellent fish; oysters are their
speciality.   £££

11e Arrondissement

Jacques Melat   42 Rue Léon-Frot
Tel. 43 70 59 27   Métro: Charonne
Open 08.00-19.30 hrs, Tues and Thurs 11.00-22.00 hrs,
closed Sun and Mon.
Rustic cooking – simple, tasty and reasonably
priced.   £

Le Thermomètre   4 Place de la République
Tel. 47 00 30 78   Métro: République
Open daily until 01.00 hrs.
Brasserie.   £

12e Arrondissement

La Connivence   1 Rue de Cotte
Tel. 46 28 46 17   Métro: Ledru Rollin
Open 12.00-14.00 hrs, 20.00-23.00 hrs
A plain, friendly bistro serving traditional
food.   £

Le Morvan   22 Rue Chaligny
Tel. 43 07 47 66   Métro: Reuilly Diderot
Open 12.00-14.15 hrs, 19.00-21.30 hrs
Closed Saturday night and Sunday
A charming bistro with Morvan regional cooking, cooked
by the owner himself.   ££

13e Arrondissement

Chez Françoise   23 Rue de la Butte aux Cailles
Tel. 45 80 12 02   Métro: Corvisart
Closed Sundays
Excellent duck pâté and cassoulet.   £

Chez Michèle   39 Rue Daviel
Tel. 45 80 09 13   Métro: Glacière
Open 10.00-15.00 hrs, 18.00-24.00 hrs
An excellent opportunity to try couscous!   ££

Les Algues   66 Ave des Gobelins
Tel. 43 31 58 22   Métro: Place d'Italie
Open 12.00-14.00 hrs, 19.30-22.30 hrs, closed
Sun/Mon.
Specialises in seafood. The menu is changed
daily.   ££

14e Arrondissement

Art et Buffet   16 Rue de la Grande Chaumière
Tel. 46 34 24 16   Métro: Vavin
Open daily until 23.30 hrs, closed Sundays
Delicious quiches and salads. Bright and
airy.   £

Hippopotamus   12 Avenue du Maine
Tel. 42 22 36 75   Métro: Montparnasse
Open until 01.00 hrs, closed between 16.00-18.30 hrs
Great steakhouse.   £

Chez Brebert   71 Bld du Montparnasse
Tel. 42 22 55 31   Métro: Montparnasse
Open until Midnight daily
Excellent couscous.   £

La Coupole   102 Bld du Montparnasse
Tel. 43 20 14 20   Métro: Vavin
Open until 02.00 hrs
A famous landmark. Notice the décor, some by Toulouse
Lautrec. Dancing in the evenings. Good
fish dishes.   ££

Bougnat Boutique   116 Ave de Général Leclerc
Tel. 45 43 98 18   Métro: Alésia
Open 11.30-14.30 hrs, 18.30-22.30 hrs
Specialises in fondues.   ££

15e Arrondissement

Le Commerce   51 Rue du Commerce
Tel. 45 75 03 27   Métro: Commerce
Open 13.00-21.45 hrs
Quick, authentic French cooking. Related to Chartier (9e
Arrondissement) but fewer tourists
here.   £

Ashoka   5 Rue Dr Jacquemarie-Clemence
Tel. 45 32 96 46   Métro: Commerce
Closed Monday lunchtime
An excellent Indian restaurant, Tandoori a
speciality.   £

Le Ciel de Paris   Montparnasse Tower, 56th Floor
Tel. 45 38 52 35   Métro: Montparnasse
Open until 23.00 hrs
Magnificent views over Paris in a romantic setting. Wise to
book in advance.   £

Au Passé Retrouvé   13 Rue Mademoiselle
Tel. 45 50 35 29   Métro: Cambronne
Open daily, closed Sunday and Monday lunch.
Wonderful atmosphere, bizarre decor and delicious
country cooking.   £

L'Orient Express   4 Ave de la Porte de Sèvres
Tel. 45 57 26 27   Métro: Balard
Closed Sunday/Monday
Serves until 22.30 hrs
This superb restaurant is an authentic carriage of this
famous train. First class service, excellent fish and
seafood.   £££

16e Arrondissement

Brasserie Stella   143 Avenue Victor Hugo
Tel. 45 53 02 68   Métro: Victor Hugo
Closed Sunday, serves until 23.30 hrs.   £

Le Cotton   73 Avenue Kléber
Tel. 47 27 73 75   Métro: Trocadero/Boissière
Open lunchtime until 23.00, closed Sunday
Good French food.   £

17e Arrondissement

Chez Natasha   35 Rue Guersant
Tel. 45 74 23 86   Métro: Ternes
Open 12.00-15.00 hrs, 19.00-24.00 hrs, closed Sunday
Buffet hors d'oeuvres, wine from the barrel.   £

Hippopotamus   46 Avenue Wagram
Tel. 46 22 16 14   Métro: Ternes/Etoile
Open until 01.00 hrs
Excellent value steaks.   £

L'Amanguier   43 Ave des Ternes
Tel. 43 80 19 28   Métro: Ternes
Open until 24.00 hrs
Lively, popular and good food.   ££

Le Relais de Venise   Corner of Bvd Pereire
Tel. 45 74 27 97   Métro: Porte Maillot
Open 12.00-14.30 hrs, 19.00-23.45 hrs
The best steaks you'll ever taste! It's steak or nothing here
but you won't wish for anything else. No reservations so
go early – it's very popular.   ££

La Marée   1 Rue Daru
Tel. 47 63 52 42   Métro: Ternes
Closed Saturdays and Sundays
Reservations recommended. Excellent crayfish, delicious
sauces.   £££

18e Arrondissement

Au Grain de Folie   24 Rue de la Vieuville
Tel. 42 58 15 57   Métro: Abbesses
Open 12.00-14.30 hrs, 19.00-23.00 hrs, closed Monday
Imaginative vegetarian dishes, warm local atmo-
sphere.   £

La Refuge des Fondues   17 Rue Trois Frères
Tel. 42 55 22 65   Métro: Abbesses
Open daily, two sittings 18.30, 20.30 hrs
Choice of meat or cheese fondue, young, lively
atmosphere. The wine is served in baby
bottles.   £

Au Clair de la Lune   9 Rue Poulbot
Tel. 42 58 97 03   Métro: Abbesses
Closed Sunday and Monday lunch
A romantic Montmartre restaurant. Nouvelle
cuisine.   ££

Wepler   14 Place de Clichy
Tel. 45 22 53 24   Métro: Place de Clichy
Open daily until 02.00 hrs
Renowned brasserie. Fresh shellfish a
speciality.   ££

Chez Plumeau   7 Place du Calvaire
Tel. 46 06 70 67   Métro: Abbesses
Open daily
Very attractive restaurant set in the heart of Montmartre.
There is a review (small play) on in the evenings so prices
go up after 22.00 hrs.
Lunch   £
Dinner   ££

Le Montmartre   74 Rue Des Martyrs
Tel. 42 51 17 45   Métro: Pigalle
Open daily until 22.30 hrs
A bubbling brasserie serving good traditional French
food.   ££

Guide to Menu Items

Les Viandes	Meat
Agneau	Lamb
Aiguillette de boeuf	Braised beef
Andouillette	Tripe
Blanquette de veau	Casseroled veal with thick, creamy sauce
Boeuf	Beef
Boeuf Bourguignon	Beef cooked in red wine
Brochettes	Spit-cooked or barbecued meat (on skewers)
Carbonnade de boeuf	Casseroled beef
Cervelle	Brains
Châteaubriant	Fillet steak
Coeur	Heart
Contrefilet	Sirloin
Côtes de boeuf	Ribs of beef
Côtes/côtelettes	Chops
Entrecôte minute	Thin steak
Entrecôte au poivre	Pepper steak
Epaule de mouton	Shoulder of lamb
Escalope de veau	Veal escalope
Escargots	Snails
Filet	Fillet
Foie	Liver
Gigot d'Agneau	Leg of lamb
Jambon	Ham
Langue	Tongue
Museau de Porc	Pig's snout
Pavé	Steak
Paupiettes de veau	Rolled stuffed veal pieces
Porc	Pork
Pot au feu	Meat & vegetable stew
Ris de veau	Sweetbreads
Rognon	Kidney
Rôti	Roast
Selle d'Agneau	Saddle of lamb
Tranche	Top of the rump (also means 'slice')
Veau	Veal

Gibier et Volaille	Game & Poultry
Bécasse	Woodcock
Caille	Quail
Canard	Duck
Chevreuil	Venison
Civet de lapin/lièvre	Jugged rabbit/hare
Coq au vin	Chicken in red wine
Faisan	Pheasant
Lapin	Rabbit
Lièvre	Hare
Oie	Goose

Perdrix	Partridge
Pintade	Guinea hen
Poulet basquaise	Basque chicken
Poussin farci	Stuffed chicken
Sanglier	Wild Boar

Les Poissons / Fish

Anguille	Eel
Brochet	Pike
Cabillaud/Morne	Cod/Salt Cod
Eperlan	Whitebait
Hareng	Herring
Maquereau	Mackerel
Merlan	Whiting
Meunière	Floured and buttered
Mulet	Mullet
Poché	Poached
Quenelles	Pike mousse/fish balls
Raie	Skate
Rouget	Red mullet
Saumon	Salmon
Sole	Sole
Thon	Tuna
Truite	Trout
Turbot	Turbot
à la vapeur	Steamed

Les Fruits de Mer / Shellfish

Belons	Type of large oyster
Bouillabaisse	Fish stew
Calamares	Squid
Coquilles St Jacques	Scallops
Crabe/Tourteau	Crab
Crevette	Shrimp
Ecrevisse	Crayfish
Fines Claires	Type of small oyster
Homard	Lobster
Huîtres	Oysters
Langouste	Lobster
Langoustine	Large prawn
Moules (marinières)	Mussels (stewed in a delicious sauce!)
Poulpe	Octopus
Praire	Clam
La soupe de poisson	Fish soup

Les Légumes / Vegetables

Ail	Garlic
Artichaut	Artichoke
Asperge	Asparagus
Betterave	Beetroot
Cèpes/Champignons	Mushroom
Choucroute	Sauerkraut

Chou-fleur	Cauliflower
Cornichon	Gherkin
Cresson	Watercress
Crudités	Salad of raw vegetables
Chips	Crisps
Endive	Chicory
Epinards	Spinach
Fenouil	Fennel
Haricots Verts	French beans
Navet	Turnip
Oignon	Onion
Petits pois	Peas
Poireau	Leek
Poivre	Pepper for seasoning
Poivron	Red/green pepper
Pommes allumettes	Thin chips
Pommes frites	Chips
Pommes de terre	Potatoes
Salade Niçoise	Salad: tuna, olive, egg, tomato etc.
Salade verte	Green salad
Truffes	Truffles

Les Desserts	**Desserts**
Ananas	Pineapple
Charlotte	Fruit interior – sponge exterior
Clafoutis	Flan
Coulis	Sauce made from strained fresh fruit
Coupe de la Maison	Usually ice cream, fruit & cream
Crêpe	Pancake
Fraise/Fraises des bois	Strawberry/wild strawberries
Framboise	Raspberry
Fruits en saison	Fruit in season
Gaufre	Waffle
Glace	Ice cream
Ile flottante	Whipped egg whites floating in a custard sauce
Marrons glacés	Puréed chestnuts
Mousse au chocolat	Chocolate mousse
Parfait	Chocolate ice cream
Pêche	Peach
Poire Belle Hélène	Pear topped with hot chocolate sauce
Pomme	Apple
Sorbet	Water ice (Parisian speciality)
Tarte aux fruits	Open fruit pie
Tarte aux pommes	Open apple pie

Les Boissons	Drinks
Café	Small black coffee
Crème/café crème	White coffee
Express	Small, very strong black coffee
Thé	Tea (without milk)
Thé au citron/au lait	Tea with lemon/milk
Le lait	Milk
Un demi	½ beer
Bière (à pression)	Beer (draught)
Vin rouge/blanc/rosé	Red/white/rosé wine
Pastis/Ricard/Anis /Anisette/Pernod	Aniseed-flavoured apéritif
Kir/Kir royal	Blackcurrant liqueur and white wine/champagne

Terms

Steak (etc): bleu	Very rare/blue
saignant	Rare
à point	Medium rare
moyen	Medium
bien cuit	Well done
L'addition s'il vous plaît	The bill please
La carte	The menu
Menu prix fixe	Fixed price menu
A la carte	Menu where you choose the dishes
Les hors d'oeuvres	Starters
Les entrées	First course
Le plat du jour	Main dish of the day

Cafés

The café is an important feature of Paris, playing a vital part in the life of the city. Nowhere else on earth are cafés so highly developed or so various or so good.

They can be used by visitors for food, a wide variety of drinks, hot, soft, and alcoholic, the toilet (for the price of a cup of coffee), for the telephone; or for simply getting a flavour of French social life and talk. You can rest your feet there, revive the children (who are welcome in ordinary cafés) or idly enjoy watching the world go by as you sip your coffee or aperitif.

In the evenings people mostly go to cafés to drink and talk, rather than to eat.

Initial Advice on Prices

There are two or frequently three tiers of prices in cafés. The cheapest is standing at the bar counter; next cheapest sitting near the bar; most expensive sitting on the terrace (or pavement in summer).

You must not order your drinks at the bar, pay for them, and then sit down (as you would in an English pub) because of the difference in prices.

Every café displays a full price list. Examine it – especially before ordering less basic drinks like non-French beers or whisky.

Cafés in side streets are generally cheaper and less busy. Cafés close to popular tourist sights are more expensive and more occupied by tourists.

Café Selection

There are more than 10,000 cafés in Paris. It is beyond the scope of this guide to begin to list the more interesting ones.

However, here are the names of a handful of some famous ones:

Les Deux Magots

170 Boulevard St-Germain (6e)
Métro: St Germain des Près
Expensive.

Le Café Flore

Boulevard St-Germain (6e)
Métro: St Germain des Près
Expensive.

La Périgourdine

Quai des Grand Augustins (5e)
Métro: St Michel
Terrific band every night after 10.00 p.m. (very expensive).

Café de la Paix

Place de l'Opéra/Bd. des Capucines (9e)
Métro: Opéra
Coffee approx 20F, wonderful ice-cream (but expensive).

Salons de Thé Selection

Angélina

226 Rue de Rivoli, 1er.
Métro: Tuileries/Concorde
10 a.m.-7 p.m., open Sundays, closed mid-July to mid-August
Provides aristocratic afternoon tea, delectable pastries, supreme hot chocolate, plus Belle Epoque décor.

Rose Thé

91 Rue St-Honoré. 1er
Métro: Louvre/Châtelet-Les-Halles

In a peaceful courtyard, surrounded by antique shops. Teas not too expensive.

La Pagode
57 Bis Rue de Babylone, 7e
Métro: St Francis-Xavier
4-10 p.m. Tea in a real and beautiful pagoda; in summer in the Chinese garden.

Tea Caddy
14 Rue St Julien-le-Pauvre
Métro: St Michel
Tea or coffee served in a very old house. In Latin Quarter, just across the bridge from Notre Dame. Moderate prices. Home-made cakes, scones and cinnamon toast.

Salon de Thé St-Louis
81 Rue St Louis-en-l'Ile, 4e
Métro: Pont-Marie
54 varieties of tea.

Christian Constant
26 Rue du Bac, 7e
Métro: Rue du Bac
8 a.m.-8 p.m.
Tea room (19 kinds served) cum pastry and chocolate shop of exceptional quality.

Drinks

A common aperitif in Paris is kir. Kir is cassis (blackcurrant liqueur) with chilled white wine. Kir royale is cassis with sparkling wine.

Gin and tonic is not a recognised aperitif in Paris and is expensive. Vermouth, dry or sweet, is often favoured, e.g. Noilly Prat (dry and white) or Dubonnet (sweet and red).

Drinks without alcohol are very popular, such as the refreshing *citron presse* (fresh lemon juice).

Chapter Ten

Nightlife and Entertainment

Paris After Dark

Paris has an international reputation for its nightlife. Apart from all the glamour, there is a sense of animation in Paris at night which is contagious.

Paris is supreme in the range and quantity of its nightly diversions – clubs, bars, discos, cabarets, revues and jazz cellars – all of which give it a unique social life, along with other forms of culture and entertainment. Here is the barest summary of the choice of activities and entertainment you can enjoy in Paris.

Strolling Around

The cheapest way to enjoy Paris after dark is to wander around and enjoy the street scenes, taking the occasional drink in sidewalk cafés. Among the more conspicuous spectacles are:
a) entertainers around the Beaubourg Centre;
b) the parade of latest fashions and exotic garb by streams of people mustering in the area of Place St-Michel and neighbouring streets (in the Latin Quarter);
c) chic and showy pageant of people in the Champs-Elysées; chic and more classic spectacle around the Opéra area; chic but also mixed and more bohemian round the cafés and clubs in St-Germain-des-Prés and Montparnasse.

The seven main areas of nightlife are to be found in Champs-Elysées, Les Halles, Opéra, Montmartre (all Right Bank); and St-Germain-des-Prés, Montparnasse, and the Latin Quarter (all Left Bank).

Clubs

Clubs are generally very lively and crowded, with dancing a feature. Some have cabaret and revue. There is also a generous choice of jazz and live rock clubs, and Paris is now the centre of new African music. Latin-American music is also popular, especially Brazilian samba.

From youthful cellar clubs in the Latin Quarter where everyone might be freely welcome, to the renowned

Régine's in the 8th arrondissement the term 'club' can cover many different styles of nightlife. Most evident of all are the 'discos' some of which are listed below.

Discothèques

The name 'discothèque' is applied widely and very loosely to many night spots. Discos range from the very stylish to the garish to the gimcrack. The more recognised ones are glitzy, supercharged, frenetic, and most often galvanising. Here is a selection.

Discothèques

Olivia Valère

40 Rue du Colisée (8e)   Tel. 42 25 11 68
Métro: Franklin D Roosevelt
140F per drink; an exclusive club.

Le Palace

8 Rue du Faubourg Montmartre (9e)   Tel. 42 46 10 87
Métro: Rue Montmartre
80F weekdays, 100F at weekends.

La Scala

188 bis Rue de Rivoli (1e)   Tel. 42 61 64 00
Métro: Palais Royal
All welcome; free for girls Mondays – Thursdays, Weekends, 80F.

Le Bus Palladiux

6 Rue Fontaine (9e)   Tel. 48 74 54 99
Métro: Blanche
Trendy place, closed Mondays. Free Entry Tuesday – Thursday, 120F Friday – Sunday.

Fifth Avenue

2 bis Avenue Foch (6e)   Tel. 45 00 00 13
Métro: Etoile
100F per drink. Exclusive club.

Le Locomotive

90 Bd de Clichy   Tel. 42 57 37 37
Métro: Blanche
Lively atmosphere, closed Mondays, 50F weekdays, 80F weekends.

Les Bains Douches

7 Rue Bourg L'Abbé (3e)   Tel. 48 87 01 80
Métro: Etienne Marcel
Fashion is the main attraction. Fun music. 100F entrance.

New York, New York

27 Rue du Cadet Mouchette (4e)   Tel. 43 21 48 96
Métro: Montparnasse
Lively music and videos, closed Mondays, 60F weekdays,
100F weekends.

Wine Bars

These are relatively new in Paris and are usually quite
crowded and lively, serving a large choice of wine.

Le Rubis

10 Rue Marché-St-Honoré (1e)
Métro: Tuileries Typically old-style Parisian, small and
bustling (reasonable prices).

L'Ecluse

Place de la Madeleine (8e)
Métro: Madeleine
Well-known (more expensive).

A la Cloche des Halles

28 Rue Coquillière (1e)
Métro: Les Halles
Marvellous choice of wines, informal (good prices).

Smart Bars

Cocktail/American-style bars are becoming very popular
in Paris. The atmosphere here is very different from the
informal style cafés. People usually dress up and go here
for drinks before (or after) a show or club. These bars
usually have a piano player and here it is possible to escape
the frantic pace of Paris by relaxing in lush, comfortable
surroundings.

Some recommendations:

The American Bar

56th Floor, Montparnasse Tower, Bd. Montparnasse
Métro: Montparnasse-Bienvenue
Approximate price for cocktails: 50-60F. Amazing views
across Paris.

L'Hôtel

13 Rue des Beaux Arts (6e)
Métro: St-Germain-des-Près
Very 'gentil' and quiet. This is where Oscar Wilde lived.

Harry's Bar

5 Rue Daunou (2e)
Métro: Opéra
Piano bar with exotic cocktails.

Paradis aux Fruits

Quai des Grand Augustins (5e)
Métro: St Michel
Very good video bar with non-alcoholic cocktails.

Les Trottoirs de Buenos Aires

37 Rue des Lombards (1e)
Métro: Châtelet
Latin American dance show. Very good fun – try the
tequila!

Cabaret Shows

Paris has been famous for its cabaret shows for a hundred
years (the Moulin Rouge opened in 1889). The best are
excellent and expensive, maintaining a superb tradition of
professional entertainment and well staged glamour.

Going to a top Parisian cabaret is a night out to
remember. There are three categories of essentially girl-
shows. One is where you see the performance just as in a
theatre (e.g. Folies Bergère). Another is where you dine
during the first performance and drink during the others
(e.g. Lido, Moulin Rouge). The other is where you just
watch and drink (Crazy Horse).

Generally, prices for the show start at 300F per person
and will include a bottle of champagne between two (or
two large drinks each). It is also possible to dine before the
show at some cabarets; prices start at 440F per person for
basic menu, half bottle of wine, show and half bottle of
champagne.

It is always necessary to make a reservation before
going.

Some top-class cabarets are the following:

Paradis Latin

28 Rue du Cardinal-Lemoine   Tel. 43 25 28 28
Métro: Cardinal Lemoine
The most Parisian show of them all. Highly recommended.
Marvellous, spontaneous and very slick, featuring a
superb can-can sequence. Probably the best show in town.

Lido

116 bis Avenue des Champs Elysées   Tel. 45 63 11 61
Métro: George V
Spectacular international cabaret featuring the Bluebell
Girls; stunning stage sets including real camels! Dinner/
Dance at 8 p.m., first show at 10 p.m., second show at
12.30 a.m.

Moulin Rouge

Place Blanche   Tel. 46 06 00 19
Métro: Blanche

Well known show featuring the 40 Doriss Girls. International revue. Dinner/Dance at 8 p.m., first show at 10 p.m., second show at midnight.

Folies-Bergère

32 Rue Richer   Tel. 42 46 77 11
Métro: Cadet
In the style of the traditional 19th century musical a mixture of variety acts and modern dance routines. One show per evening at 21.00.

The Crazy Horse Saloon

12 Avenue George V   Tel. 47 23 32 32
Métro: George V
World-famous erotic (but tasteful) show.

Opera and ballet and concerts

Tickets for opera and ballet at the Opera House are extremely difficult to obtain. You can see the magnificent interior of the Opera House during the day (for a small charge).

Classical music concerts are plentiful, some given in historic churches: see current listings. Also there are other less exalted venues for ballet and dance theatre and opera, especially during the many festivals held in Paris.

Cinema and Theatre

Paris has the widest and most numerous choice of films. Most foreign films are shown in the original: VO (*version originale*) means with French sub-titles. Unless you are a true linguist avoid films marked VF: this means they are dubbed in French.

Theatre is very varied – but you need French for it.

Chapter Eleven

Children in Paris

Paris is welcoming to children, but Parisians expect children to be better behaved than Americans or British people do.

Here are some places and entertainments of special interest to children.

Parks and Playgrounds

Jardin d'Acclimation, 16e.

Métro: Porte Maillot/Sablons

In the Bois de Boulogne, at the northern edge. A 25 acre amusement park. You can take a miniature train to it from Porte Maillot (afternoon only). The best children's playground in Paris. A very wide variety of activities and facilities – fairground, adventure playgrounds, animals, miniature farm, rides, house of mirrors, etc. Sure bet for pre-teenage child. Open 10.00-18.30 hrs (Sunday to 19.30 hrs).

Bois de Vincennes

Métro: Porte Dorée

Has the best zoo in the city – an enjoyable zoo. Open daily 9.00-17.30 hrs. Also, on the other (eastern) side of the wood, is the Paris Flower Garden (Parc Floral). A miniature train tours the gardens, and there's a children's play area, and on summer weekends, clowns, puppets, etc.

The Bois de Vincennes is a large recreational area with an expanse of woodland, boating lake, museums, and a classical château – there is as much for adults to enjoy as in the Bois de Boulogne.

The Musée des Arts Africains et Océaniens (near the Zoo) should interest older children (8 plus) and adults. Downstairs, too, there is a marvellous tropical aquarium.

Many of the parks in the centre of Paris have children's play and amusement parks – though rather too ordered. Best provided is the *Luxembourg Gardens* – playground, donkey rides, pond for toy boats, puppets. Also note the Tuileries garden for some similar facilities.

The gardens of the Champs-de-Mars – with the Eiffel Tower next to them – have a children's playground and donkey rides.

Museums

Grévin Museum

The main Grévin museum (Boulevard Montmartre, 9e) waxworks, with some fun ideas and shows. Should be a sure success for children.

Museum of Popular Arts and Traditions

In the Bois de Boulogne – has lots of displays for children to operate.

La Villette

See Chapter 5 for children's play areas. The great science museum, the City of Science and Industry, should hold the attention of older children (12 plus). The Géode cinema is likely to amaze one and all.

Toy Shops

Au Nain Bleu

406-401 Rue Saint-Honoré, 8e
Métro: Concorde/Madeleine
A famous toyshop, worth goggling at. Small children will
be thrilled by a walk round the store. But luxury prices.

Ali-Baba

29 Avenue de Tourville, 7e
Métro: Ecole-Militaire
Three storeys of toys for all ages.

Babysitters

Babysitters cost about 40 francs per hour. Your hotel will
usually be able to arrange for this. There are several
established agencies, including:

Ababa, La Maman en Plus

Tel. 43 22 22 11

Includes English speakers.

General Association of Paris Medical Students

Tel. 45 86 19 42

Maman Poule

Tel. 47 47 78 78

Chapter Twelve

Being City-Wise and Street-Wise

Tipping

Tipping is widely practised and is done with panache.

Hotels and restaurants: 15% service is included in the bill.
For hotel staff, see Chapter 2. It is common but optional to
leave something extra for the waiter: if you are pleased, say
5-10%. For service at the counter in cafés and bars, leave
small change.

Guides: Museum and tour guides should be tipped: about
5F for a museum tour; about 10% for an excursion
(depending upon length, and numbers of tourists and so
on).

Taxi Drivers: 10-15%.

Cloakroom Attendants: About 2F.

Lost Property

Lost Property Office – address:
Bureau des Objets Trouvés
36 Rue des Morillons, 15e.
Métro: Convention
Open Monday to Friday 8.30-17.00 (Thursday until 20.00).

Left Luggage Facilities

Left luggage facilities are available at all mainline stations and at Porte Maillot Air France bus terminal.

Left luggage can be left at the *consigne* (Left Luggage Office) for approximately 10F per day. Left luggage lockers are available at approximately 5F per day.

Safety and Security

Pickpocketing and bag-snatching are rife in many tourist areas.

Handbags should be kept fastened securely. They should be carried in a way which cannot easily be snatched such as over the opposite shoulder, across the body.

Wallets should never be carried in a pickable pocket. Be particularly careful in crowded places such as the Métro. Pickpockets frequently work in pairs, taking advantage of crowds to jostle and distract their victims while stealing a purse or wallet.

Among the most skilful thieves are groups of gipsy children who roam the main tourist areas of Paris and the Métro. Do not stop if approached by these children and never take out your purse or wallet to give them anything, as it may be snatched.

If you have something of value stolen, report the theft to the nearest police station and obtain an *attestation de vol* (an official declaration of theft for insurance purposes). It will be easier if you are accompanied, especially by someone who speaks French well.

Women on their own can be perfectly comfortable and safe in Paris, in cafés and on the street. This applies to areas where numbers of people are present (and which are not clearly disreputable). The Bois de Boulogne is not safe at night. Do not be uneasy if you are stared at during the day: it is not rude to look intently at a pretty or interesting face in France.

Police

The ordinary police are the gendarmes, who wear blue uniforms and *képi* hats. Address a gendarme with *Pardon, Monsieur l'agent*.

Daily Hours

Shops stay open until 18.30 or 19.30 hrs; some smaller ones close for an hour at lunch. Sunday is a standard closing day (many food shops open), and also Monday for some neighbourhood shops and food shops.

Paris city centre is far less crowded mid-morning than in the afternoon. Morning, near opening time, is the best time to visit museums and the department stores.

Most museums close at 17.00-18.00 hrs.

Traffic is most congested in the centre from 16.30 hrs onwards, slowing buses and taxis. The Métro is packed between 17.00 and 19.00 hrs with the office rush hour.

Nightlife – clubs and discos and bars – begins late, around 22.00 or 23.00 hrs. The Métro finishes about 00.45 hrs. Much nightlife will go on until about 02.00 hrs, and a sprinkling of devoted nightlife until dawn.

Sundays and Public Holidays

Museums and restaurants are mostly open on public holidays and also on Sundays.

Sunday services are held in Notre Dame Cathedral at 8.00, 8.45, 10.00 (Mass), 11.30, 12.30, and 20.30 hrs. There is an organ recital every Sunday at 19.45 hrs.

The main public holidays are: Jan 1; Easter Sunday and Monday; Ascension Day; Whit Monday; Bastille Day (July 14); Assumption (August 15); All Saints (Nov 1); Armistice Day (Nov 11); Christmas Day.

Seasonal Paris

One should visit Paris in every season to enjoy its different aspects.

Winter: best season for nightlife and shows. Very good for shopping (and real bargains in January sales). The period leading up to Christmas is bad for traffic jams, and quite tremendous for shop window displays. Many Parisians leave the city over the Christmas holidays. Museums rather less crowded.

Summer: Paris is at its quietest between July 15th and August 25th, when many Parisians are on holiday. Summer is a good time to wander the Paris streets and to discover its buildings. August can be sultry, however.

Spring and Autumn: Paris at its most typical. Spring for a sense of romance; autumn for nostalgia. The Paris light at its most beautiful.

La Politesse – Manners and Etiquette

The French are considerably more formal than the Americans or British. Manners matter.

On entering a small shop, or acknowledging someone, it is polite to say *Bonjour Monsieur* or *Madame*. Note that 'Bonjour' by itself is insufficient; always say 'Bonjour Monsieur', etc. When addressing someone, *Monsieur* and *Madame* may be used without the surname. *Madame* is used for an older woman; *Mademoiselle* is used for a young woman or girl.

Say that with a smile and you are off to the right start. Use whenever appropriate the other standard phrases of politeness: *s'il vous plaît* for please, again always followed by *monsieur* or *madame*; *excusez-moi*, etc.

Don't hesitate to shake hands, briskly and firmly. It is common practice when meeting someone or saying good-bye. Try to use whatever French you can to express your pleasure and regard.

You can dress informally, except for top class restaurants, when ties and suits are expected; cabaret restaurants (where some people will be wearing evening dress) and for private clubs, not conservatively but appropriately. You should dress respectfully before entering churches (it is not necessary to cover your head).

Language

Language — Le Français

You should acquire at least some few phrases of French, both for your own needs and for *la politesse*.

The main difficulty for someone quite ignorant of French is more in pronunciation than in vocabulary. Try to get help and practice with pronunciation at any opportunity – from friends, couriers, perhaps your children at school. There are excellent introductory programmes on radio and TV (enquire to the BBC).

There are some characteristic French sounds which once you have got them, will very greatly ease your way in speaking French. Some people advocate that the way to acquire the trick of imitating French sounds is to mimic a strong French accent whilst speaking English. Try this out with anyone who will play.

It is worth getting a simple pocket French phrase book if your French is non-existent or very slight.

Chapter Thirteen

Sunday in Paris

There is plenty going on in Paris on a Sunday but if you should find yourself at a loose end, here are a few suggestions:

Excursions

A variety of excursions are available in Paris on a Sunday. Please check once in Paris for details.

Shops and Markets

Certain shops on the Rue de Rivoli, Champs Elysées and at Les Halles open on Sundays.

The Marché aux Puces (flea market), Marché aux Oiseaux (bird market) and many other markets are open on Sundays. See 'Shopping' section for details.

'Bouquinistes', the small picture and book stalls down by the river Seine are often open on Sundays and provide interesting browsing.

Museums and Galleries

A number of museums and galleries are either half price or free on Sundays. A good guide to this is a publication called 'L'Officiel des Spectacles' available from newsagents (cost: 2F). Look up 'Musées' – 'Dim gratuit' means free on Sundays or 'Demi-tariff le dim' is half price. This also gives opening hours and costs.

Eating and Drinking

You can of course eat and drink all day in Paris but two Sunday specials are:

Bertillon Ice Creams: these famous ice creams can be enjoyed at Bertillon's, Rue St Louis en L'Ile. Métro: Pont Marie.

Tea at Angelinas, 226 Rue de Rivoli, Tel. 42 60 82 00 – The place to be seen having afternoon tea on Sunday!

Church Services

Anglican
St Georges Church
7 Rue Auguste-Vacquerie 16e   Tel. 47 20 22 51
Métro: George V/Kleber
Main Sunday service 8.30 and 10.30 hrs.

British Embassy Church (St Michael's)
5 Rue d'Aguesseau (8e)   Tel. 47 42 70 88
Métro: Concorde/Madeleine
Main Sunday services 08.30, 10.30, 11.30, 18.30 hrs.

You could of course take the opportunity of attending a service in any of the French Churches in Paris. These are mainly Catholic but services are of course open to all denominations.

Sunday services are held in:
Notre Dame Cathedral
Métro: City
At 08.00, 08.45, 10.00 Mass, 11.30, 12.30 and 18.30 hrs with an organ recital each Sunday at 17.45 hrs.

Sacré Coeur Montmartre
Métro: Abbesses
Sunday services are held at 07.00, 08.00, 09.00, 09.45, 11.00 Mass and 12.30 hrs.

Parks and Gardens

A good solution if the weather's fine and you'd like a little exercise, space and air! See Chapter 6 – Sights and Places to See.

Cinema

Many films in Paris are shown in their original language. 'L'Officiel des Spectacles' or 'Pariscope' (available from newsagents, 2F) are good guides (and good for your French!). Most films you will recognise by their titles or by the actors. The letters VO (version originelle) in brackets after the cinema name means that the film is in its original language.

Chapter Fourteen

At Your Service

Money, Currency Exchange, and Banks

French currency

The unit of French currency is the franc (usually written F or f). The franc is divided into 100 centimes.

The exchange rate between the franc and the pound sterling over the recent period has averaged, very approximately, 10 francs to £1. (It has been around 7 francs to the US dollar). Check the exchange rate more precisely at the time of your trip.

The following French currency denominations are in circulation.

Coins: 5, 10, and 20 centimes. All copper coloured.
50 centimes (½F – silver coloured).
2 and 5 francs (silver coloured).
10 francs (bronze coloured)
Notes: 20, 50, 100, 200, and 500 francs.

Amounts in francs are written as follows in this guidebook:

15.25F or 15F25 – denoting 15 francs 25 centimes.

What to take with you

It pays to change sterling for French francs before you leave Britain and take francs with you. In any case you should have some French francs with you to tide you over the first day.

Changing Money

You can change money and cheques at banks, exchange bureaux (Bureau de Change) and larger hotels. You will be required to produce your passport for all transactions except when changing cash. Commission rates vary and can be high in the case of hotels. Generally, banks deduct a flat sum as commission, making it uneconomic to change small sums of money.

Travellers' Cheques are a safe way of carrying money but may be more difficult to change over a weekend.

Eurocheques can usually be cashed for francs at French banks which display the Eurocheque symbol. Your cheques must be presented with a Eurocheque card (a special card for use abroad which must be obtained from your bank in advance) and passport. Production of a normal cheque card, even with a Eurocheque symbol displayed in the corner, will no longer be accepted abroad.

N.B. If you do use your Eurocheque card, the maximum amount you can cash in any one day is 1,200 francs. If you use your Eurocheque card to cash a cheque in Paris on your last day abroad, you will not be allowed to do so the same day in the U.K. because of the £50 limit.

Banks

Normal opening hours: 9.00-16.30 hrs, Monday to Friday. Banks close at 12.00 hrs on the eve of national holidays. Smaller branches close for lunch between 12.00 and 14.00 hrs.

British Banks

Barclays
33 Rue du Quatre Septembre (9e)   Tel. 42 65 65 65

157 Bvd St-Germain (6e)   Tel. 42 22 28 63

6 Rond Point des Champs Elysées (8e) Tel. 43 59 15 26

106 bis Rue St Lazare (8e)   Tel. 45 22 97 72

24 Avenue Kléber (8e)   Tel. 45 00 86 86

Open 09.00-16.30 hrs Monday-Friday. You can obtain from 500F (minimum) up to your Barclaycard (Visa) limit or cash two £50 cheques with your cheque book, cheque card and passport if you bank with Barclays.

Midland
6 Rue Piccini, 75016   Tel. 45 02 80 80

Open 09.00-16.00 hrs. Monday-Friday. You can cash two £50 cheques with a Eurocheque card and your passport. (A charge of 31F per cheque is made for this.) Eurocheques are also accepted.

National Westminster
18 Place Vendôme (1e)   Tel. 42 60 37 40

Open: 09.00-16.00 hrs. Monday-Friday, closed: 12.00-14.00 hrs.
National Westminster cheques are accepted here and the £50 limit does not apply. The bank will telephone your bank in England for a statement of your account, and will then give you the money you need (a charge of 100F is made for this). Eurocheques are accepted; the limit on these is 1200F. Access taken.

Lloyds
43 Bvd des Capucines (2e)   Tel. 42 61 51 25
Open 09.00-16.00 hrs Monday-Friday.

Exchange Bureaux and Banks Open Outside Normal Banking Hours

Charles de Gaulle Airport
6.00-23.00 hrs daily.
   Exchange bureaux are open every day at the following railway stations:

Gare du Nord (6.30-22.00 hrs).
Gare de Lyon (7.00-23.00 hrs).
Gare de l'Est, Gare St Lazare, Gare d'Austerlitz (all 7.00-21.00 hrs, except Sunday).
Gare Montparnasse (9.00-19.00 hrs).

   The exchange bureaux at the railway stations are a last resort, as they are usually crowded and irksome. It is worth making sure that you do not run short of francs and need currrency exchange facilities at the weekend or out of normal banking hours.

Credit Cards

American Express, Diners Club, and Barclaycard Visa are accepted in many shops and restaurants in Paris, Access less widely.
   To change money on Access you must go to the Crédit Agricole at either of the following addresses:

14 Rue de la Boëtie, (8e),   Tel. 42 65 00 32
Métro: St Augustin
Open 9.30-13.30, 14.45-17.30 hrs Monday-Friday.

16 bis Bd de Sebastopol, (4e),   Tel. 42 78 03 54
Métro: Châtelet
Open 9.15-17.00 hrs Monday to Saturday.

To change money on Visa:-

Crédit Commercial de France
115 Champs Elysées, (8e),
Métro: Charles de Gaulle-Etoile
Open 8.30-20.00 hrs daily.
   In both cases, you will probably be required to produce your passport.

Post and Telephone

The postal and telephone service is known as PTT (pronounced 'pay tay tay').
   Post Office hours: 8-19.00 hrs. Monday-Friday; 9.00-12.00 hrs. Saturday.
   The Central Post Office is at 52 Rue du Louvre, 75001

Paris. It is open 24 hours every day for telephone and telegraph (until 7 p.m. for other services). (Métro: Louvre.)

Stamps (*timbres*) are obtainable at Post Office (*bureaux de poste*) and at *tabacs* and hotels.

Telephones

You can make calls from any post office; you pay after the call.

You can phone through the switchboard of your hotel; the hotel will charge for the call at a higher rate.

You can use a payphone. If you use a payphone often, buy a phonecard or Télécarte (40F or 90F), available as for stamps; this lets you use many more public telephones in working order.

International Calls

To make a call abroad, look at the code book to see if the country can be dialled direct and note its code number (i.e. USA 1, UK 44). Here is how to proceed. To call UK from payphones which can be found at most post offices:

1. Lift receiver.
2. Insert at least 3F in coins, which gives you 1 minute.
3. Dial 19 and wait for change of tone.
4. Dial 44 (the international code for the UK) plus the appropriate UK local code, less the initial 0; e.g. to call Bristol (dialling code 0272) 12345, dial 19 44 272 12345.
5. Should you hear any recorded announcements in French, this probably means either that you have dialled the wrong number or that the lines are engaged.
6. A flashing black and white disc at the top left of the coinbox will indicate that you need to insert more coins to continue your call.

Calls Within Paris

Insert 1F (where relevant) and dial the number (eight digits).

Calls to other parts of France

1. Dial 16 and wait for a change of tone.
2. Dial the town code and the number.
3. A map and colour key in the booth gives the duration for 0.50F.

Reverse Charge Calls (known as PCV)

Dial 100 and ask operator for the number.

Note that there are cheaper evening rates and very much cheaper rates at night and on Sundays.

Medical Matters

You should take out personal travel insurance to cover any medical expenses. This will also cover theft, loss of luggage, etc.

Visitors from other EEC countries are entitled to medical treatment under the French social security system. But to qualify, you must have the necessary documentation with you. If you are a British citizen, you need to obtain Form E111 from the Department of Health and Social Security. Allow over a month to apply for this form and receive it.

In France, you pay for medical treatment at the time and about 75 per cent of the cost is refunded by the French social security.

On a short visit to France, it is better to use a private insurance policy than Form E111 and social security.

Should you consult a doctor, keep the receipt and any prescription to claim a refund from your insurance.

Doctors

The fee for a straightforward visit to a doctor is about 100F.

If you need an English-speaking doctor for important or urgent problems, contact:

SOS Médecins (24 hours; house visits)
Tel. 43 37 77 77 or 47 07 77 77
(Address: 87 Boulevard Port-Royal, 13e. RER: Port Royal)

Dentists

For urgent dental treatment:

SOS Dentistes (24 hours; house visits)
Tel. 43 37 51 00 or 45 35 41 41
(Same address as SOS Médecins)

The American Hospital also has a dental clinic open 24 hours a day: see under Hospitals, below.

Pharmacists or Chemists

Pharmacies will help with minor ailments and first aid.
Some English-speaking pharmacies are:

Pharmacie Anglaise des Champs-Elysées
62 Avenue des Champs-Elysées, 8e
Tel. 43 59 22 52
Métro: George V
Open: 8.30-22.30 hrs. Monday to Saturday.

British-American Pharmacy
1 Rue Auber, 9e
Métro: Opéra
Open: 8.30-22.00 hrs. Monday to Saturday.

Pharmacie des Arts
106 Boulevard Montparnasse, 14e   Tel. 43 25 44 88
Métro: Vavin
Open: 8.00-24.00 hrs Monday to Saturday; 9.00-13.00
hrs. Sunday and public holidays.

Hospitals

Hospitals with English-speaking staff are:

American Hospital
63 Boulevard Victor-Hugo, Neuilly   Tel. 47 47 53 00
Métro: Pont de Levallois
Outpatients: 9.00-18.00 hrs; Emergency service 24 hours
daily.

British Hospital
3 Rue Barbès, Levallois-Perret   Tel. 47 58 13 12
Métro: Anatole-France.

Useful Addresses and Telephone Numbers

The main Police Station with an interpreting service is:
Préfecture de Police, Bureau 1520, Ile de la Cité, 4e
Tel. 42 77 11 00, ext 4874.
Open daily 9.00-17.00 hrs.

Embassies

UK Embassy:
35 Rue de Faubourg St-Honoré, 8e
Tel. 42 66 91 42

USA:
2 Av Gabriel, 8e
Tel. 42 96 12 02

Australia:
4 Rue Jean-Ray, 15e
Tel. 40 59 33 00

Canada:
35 Av Montaigne, 8e
Tel. 47 23 01 01

Ireland:
12 Av Foch, 16e
Tel. 45 00 20 87

New Zealand:
7 Rue Léonard-de-Vinci, 16e
Tel. 45 00 24 11

Emergency Services:

Police: Tel. 17
Fire: Tel. 18
Ambulance (SAMU): 45 67 50 50

Chapter Fifteen

A Pick of Paris

Here is a varied selection of special recommendations that might well appeal even to those who know Paris well. Each entry is the best we know, inside a reasonable price limit.

Everything here is exceptional; and also everything here is truly representative of Paris.

At the end of your Paris city break, why not compile your own listing?

Best Bus Route

Bus No. 24. A superb route for great sights and the river Seine.

This goes from Gare St Lazare, round the Place de la Madeleine (luxury food shops), into Place de la Concorde, along the Seine by the Tuileries gardens, and past the Louvre. There's a view across the river of fine buildings – the Mint (called Hôtel des Monnaies) and the Institut de France (home of the immortal Academie Française). The bus crosses the river on the Pont Neuf to the Ile de la Cité, the island on which Notre-Dame stands, past the law courts (Palais de Justice), and crosses over the Petit Pont to the Left Bank.

It goes eastwards through part of the Boulevard St-Germain and along the Quai St Bernard beside the Seine. If you want to go back on a 24 bus, get off on the Quai St Bernard by the Jardin des Plantes (long before the terminus). Divert yourself into these gardens if you wish. On the return journey, the 24 bus goes along the left bank of the Seine, giving a splendid view of Notre Dame, and passing the corner of the Musée d'Orsay. It crosses the river by Pont Royale and returns to St Lazare by way of Concorde and the glorious rue Royale.

Métro for starting terminus: Gare St Lazare; for return bus stop: Gare d'Austerlitz.

Best View

La Samaritaine Department Store, 1er
Rue de la Monnaie (between Pont Neuf and rue de Rivoli).
  Best 360-degree view of Paris.

The store occupies four separate grand buildings. Enter Magasin 2 (Store 2) and take elevator to 9th floor, where you can have a drink in the café.

Go upstairs to 10th floor where there is a roof terrace with a matchless panorama of Paris and stunning views over the river Seine.

Six Other Great Views

Eiffel Tower, 7e   See Chapter 5.
The highest panorama: from its summit level platform you can see 50 miles on a clear day. If it's cloudy you may see Paris better from the second stage level. Note the lift is expensive.

Arc de Triomphe, 8e   See Chapter 5.
There is a uniquely satisfying view from the top of the Arc de Triomphe, with the twelve great avenues radiating from the Place Charles de Gaulle, and views to Montmartre and the Pantheon.

Pompidou Centre (or Beaubourg), 4e.   See Chapter 5.
Superbly interesting views of Paris from the free escalator that goes up the outside of the building in a transparent caterpillar tube; and also from the top floor self-service restaurant.

Tour Montparnasse (Montparnasse Tower), 14e.
This is the only skyscraper in central Paris. The best thing is that from the top you can see the rest of Paris but not this alien building which is an eyesore visible from everywhere else in Paris. The 56th Floor has a viewing gallery (with spoken commentary in English) and bar and restaurant. The lift shoots you up in 38 seconds. You can reach the open roof terrace, upstairs two floors higher. The view makes an interesting variation to that from a similar height at the top of the Eiffel Tower. It's a much more pleasant way of having the view than using the Eiffel Tower.
Open: 9.30-22.30 hrs. Summer; 10.00-22.00 hrs. Winter.
Cost: 26th Floor, 23.50F; 59th Floor, 29.50F.
Métro: Montparnasse Bienvenue.

Notre-Dame, 4e. (Chapter 5)
From one of the fastest lifts in Europe at Montparnasse we go to worn and winding stairs of the cathedral. A strenuous climb rewards you with a closer look at the gargoyles and griffins as well as a thrilling view of Paris. The South Tower offers the better view. Also, in this tower hangs the great 13-ton bell immortalised by Victor Hugo and known to millions far from France through Charles Laughton's acting as the hunchback Quasimodo. It is 252 steps to the Grande Galerie and another 90 to the South Tower.

Entrance to *Tours* (Towers) on north of cathedral in Rue Cloître-Notre-Dame, every day except Tuesday, cost 22F. Métro: Cité.

Montmartre, 18e.

The hill of Montmartre offers some of the most attractive and romantic views of Paris, especially spellbinding at dawn or dusk. Look from the steps of the Sacré-Coeur (see chapter five), or for a larger panorama climb to the dome from which you can see across virtually the whole city.

Métro: Anvers/Abbesses.

The most interesting and the most satisfying view is not the highest. The expanse of the highest views is had at the cost of detail and form. For sheer beauty, the views of Paris from the quays and bridges around the Ile Saint-Louis and the Ile de la Cité are among the greatest in Paris. Note in particular the views from the Tournelle Bridge (Pont de la Tournelle) and from the Quai d'Orléans on the Ile Saint-Louis. Also, behind the Quai de Montebello on the Left Bank, the remarkable view from Square Viviani, one of the most appealing and inspiring in Paris.

For two superb views of monumental Paris, note the terrace of the Palais de Chaillot and the Alexandre III bridge (see Chapter 6).

Most Magnificent Square

Place de la Concorde, 8e. See Chapter 5.

The greatest square in the world in the most glorious and dazzling setting. To appreciate it best get to its centre, preferably when the traffic is less, such as early on Sunday morning.

Most Picturesque Square

Place des Vosges, 4e.

The most beautiful square in Paris, and the oldest (built 1612). An unspoiled, authentic Parisian antique. In the Marais district.

Métro: St-Paul; Chemin-Vert.

Most Fashionable Square

Place des Victoires, 2e.

This circular *place* or square (built in the 17th century) has recently become a hub of new fashion. Modish boutiques and restaurants have blossomed in its noble mansions. This is where it's at, as the saying is.

Métro: Bourse.

Most Opulent Square

Place Vendôme, 1er.

A fine and very grand square set apart by wealth: here are great jewellers, perfumiers, art dealers, bankers, and the Ritz Hotel.

Métro: Tuileries.

Finest Lingerie

Nina Ricci, 8e   39 Avenue Montaigne

Here is some of the world's most beautiful lingerie. Also other feminine accoutrements and an impeccably Parisian dress collection. (If you venture beyond the ground floor with its fabulous prices and exclusive air, there is a bargain basement with big discounts.)

If the ambience here is found too daunting, there is a superlative lingerie department at Galeries Lafayette, the department store in the Boulevard Haussmann.

Best Dresses and High Fashion

Fashion Museum (Musée National des Arts de la Mode)

Pavilion de Marson   107 Rue de Rivoli, 1er

Opened in 1986, surprisingly this is the first collection in Paris to be devoted to fashion. The collection has over 10,000 costumes from the 17th century to the *à la mode* of our time. It is housed in the Marson Pavilion of the Louvre (next to the Museum of Decorative Arts). Start by taking the lift to the 5th Floor where there is a splendid view of the Tuileries gardens, and walk down.

There is a museum boutique which is a strong tip for presents: paper dolls, postcards, scarves, etc., and a beret with instructions showing four ways to wear this classic French headgear.

Open: Wednesday to Saturday, 12.30-18.00 hrs; Sunday 11.00-18.00 hrs.

Métro: Palais-Royal/Châtelet.

Best Jazz

New Morning   7-9 Rue des Petites-Ecuries, 10e

The best jazz club and, together with Ronnie Scott's, the best in Europe. Comfortable and spacious with good sound and visibility and the premier place for visiting American musicians of every jazz style.

Open 9 p.m.-13.30 hrs. Tel. 47 43 82 58

Métro: Château-d'Eau.

Most Elegant Afternoon Tea

The Lancaster Hotel   7 Rue de Berri, 8e

Delicate cucumber sandwiches, scones and cakes served in lovely surroundings: in the drawing room or in the courtyard in summer. The hotel still retains the atmosphere of a fine private house, which it was formerly.

Best Old-Fashioned Afternoon Tea

The Tea Caddy　　　　14 Rue St-Julien-le-Pauvre, 5e
　Cinnamon toast, crumpets, scones – it would be difficult to find better in England. Served in a very old house with wood panelling. Refined, but moderate prices. In Latin Quarter, just across the bridge from Notre-Dame.

Métro: St-Michel.

Best Hot Chocolate

Angélina　　　　　　　226 Rue de Rivoli, 1er
　The *chocolat chaud* (hot chocolate) is unsurpassed anywhere. Angélina's is the pre-eminent tea salon in Paris. You should not miss eating its Mont Blanc, a concoction of chestnut cream purée and meringue. But the choice in cakes and pastries is boggling.

Métro: Tuileries/Concorde.

Best Fish and Chips

Hamilton's Noted Fish and Chips

　　　　　　　　　　　51 Rue de Lappe, 11e
　All the fish and chip essentials generously supplied; take-away or eat in the shop with a good choice of English beer.
　Open: Mon-Sat 12.00-14.00 hrs., 18.00-23.30 hrs.; Sunday 18.00-23.00 hrs.

Métro: Bastille.

Best Fast Food

Crêpe Stall, 6e
　At the corner of Place St-André-des-Arts and Place St-Michel. True sophistication in fast food looked after by a woman who has been many a year in the crêpe business. A real French service.

Métro: St-Michel.

The Greatest Food Shop

Fauchon, 8e　　　　26 Place de Madeleine
　The most celebrated food store in the world and the best. A wonderful treat even if you just look. Fauchon could also be put forward for the prize window display: at its perfection in the early morning, this is a visual feast not to be missed. An astonishing composition.
　If you want to buy, the shop is expensive but a treasure house for presents. However, across the road is Fauchon's stand-up café where prices are moderate for superlative home-made cakes etc., and the most excellent coffee (or tea). A recognised institution for Parisians – but don't depend on courtesies for tourists.

Métro: Madeleine.

Best and Most Cheese

Androuet, 8e   41 rue d'Amsterdam

The foremost Paris temple to cheese. Look with wonder at the variety of cheeses on display in this store, all kept in perfect condition. At noon and 7 p.m. you can have a remarkable 2½ hour course in cheese tasting and cheese lore, for a small price – but it's all in French. It is also a cheese restaurant where you can have a 4 course meal of cheeses!

Métro: Saint-Lazare.

Best Ice Cream

Berthillon, 4e   31 Rue St-Louis-en-l'Ile

No better ice cream known, but better service can be had – at Berthillon's you queue for the best and it is part of its special prestige.

Open Wednesday to Sunday 10.00-20.00 hrs, but closed in August at the height of the ice cream season and also during some school holidays.

If you want to eat Berthillon's ice cream without queueing, go round the corner, also on the Ile Saint Louis, to La Flore en l'Ile, 42 Quai d'Orleans.

This sunny tea room also has good views of the Pantheon on the Left Bank, and of Notre Dame.

Also available at Lady Jane on Quai d'Orléans.

Métro: Pont-Marie.

Best Children's Slide

In the Parc de la Villette, 18e   Dragon Slide

A slide shaped as a dragon, 35 yards long. Child enters at the tail, crawls through the undulating belly, and slides out to emerge from the fiery mouth. For La Villette, see Chapter 5.

Métro: Porte de la Villette.

Best Park Bench, 8e

In the gardens of the Champs-Elysées there is a path named Allée Marcel Proust. Proust, the great novelist, played here. He mentions this bench in his masterpiece, and it is a good place to contemplate the pleasure of being in Paris.

Best Garden Retreat

Musée Rodin, 7e (See Chapter 6)

For a haven, go into the garden of the Rodin museum, Les Invalides. The repose of the garden is enhanced by the sculptor's works, and the lovely mansion that houses the museum itself.

Best Sunset

Go to the Square du Vert-Galant on the Ile de la Cité, which is a little green park on the western tip of the island. From there watch the sun set on the Pont des Arts.

Métro: Pont Neuf.